D1569908

Miracles

INTERPRETATION

Resources for the Use of Scripture in the Church

INTERPRETATION

RESOURCES FOR THE USE OF SCRIPTURE IN THE CHURCH

Samuel E. Balentine, *Series Editor*
Ellen F. Davis, *Associate Editor*
Richard B. Hays, *Associate Editor*
Susan E. Hylen, *Associate Editor*
Brent A. Strawn, *Associate Editor*
Patrick D. Miller, *Consulting Editor*

OTHER AVAILABLE BOOKS IN THE SERIES

LUKE TIMOTHY JOHNSON

Miracles

God's Presence and Power in Creation

INTERPRETATION *Resources for the Use of Scripture in the Church*

WESTMINSTER
JOHN KNOX PRESS
LOUISVILLE · KENTUCKY

© 2018 Luke Timothy Johnson

First edition
Published by Westminster John Knox Press
Louisville, Kentucky

18 19 20 21 22 23 24 25 26 27—10 9 8 7 6 5 4 3 2 1

All rights reserved. No part of this book may be reproduced or transmitted in any form or by any means, electronic or mechanical, including photocopying, recording, or by any information storage or retrieval system, without permission in writing from the publisher. For information, address Westminster John Knox Press, 100 Witherspoon Street, Louisville, Kentucky 40202-1396. Or contact us online at www.wjkbooks.com.

Except as otherwise indicated, Scripture quotations are from the New Revised Standard Version of the Bible, copyright © 1989 by the Division of Christian Education of the National Council of the Churches of Christ in the U.S.A., and are used by permission.

Scripture quotations marked RSV are from the Revised Standard Version of the Bible, copyright © 1946, 1952, 1971, and 1973 by the Division of Christian Education of the National Council of the Churches of Christ in the U.S.A., and are used by permission.

Scripture taken from the Holy Bible, New International Version, NIV, copyright © 1973, 1978, 1984 by International Bible Society. Used by permission of Zondervan. All rights reserved worldwide.

Scripture taken from the New King James Version®. Copyright © 1982 by Thomas Nelson. Used by permission. All rights reserved.

Book design by Drew Stevens
Cover design by designpointinc.com

Library of Congress Cataloging-in-Publication Data
Names: Johnson, Luke Timothy, author.
Title: Miracles : God's presence and power in creation / Luke Timothy Johnson.
Description: Louisville, Kentucky : Westminster John Knox Press, 2018. |
    Series: Interpretation: resources for the use of scripture in the church |
    Includes bibliographical references and index. |
Identifiers: LCCN 2018002994 (print) | LCCN 2018011746 (ebook) |
    ISBN 9781611648393 (ebk.) | ISBN 9780664234072 (hbk. : alk. paper)
Subjects: LCSH: Miracles.
Classification: LCC BT97 (ebook) | LCC BT97 .J64 2018 (print) | DDC 231.7/3—dc23
LC record available at https://lccn.loc.gov/2018002994

♾ The paper used in this publication meets the minimum requirements of the American National Standard for Information Sciences—Permanence of Paper for Printed Library Materials, ANSI Z39.48-1992.

Most Westminster John Knox Press books are available at special quantity discounts when purchased in bulk by corporations, organizations, and special-interest groups. For more information, please e-mail SpecialSales@wjkbooks.com.

To my dear wife Joy
in gratitude for the miracle of her love

CONTENTS

SERIES FOREWORD

This series of volumes supplements Interpretation: A Bible Commentary for Teaching and Preaching. The commentary series offers an exposition of the books of the Bible written for those who teach, preach, and study the Bible in the community of faith. This new series is addressed to the same audience and serves a similar purpose, providing additional resources for the interpretation of Scripture, but now dealing with features, themes, and issues significant for the whole rather than with individual books.

The Bible is composed of separate books. Its composition naturally has led its interpreters to address particular books. But there are other ways to approach the interpretation of the Bible that respond to other characteristics and features of the Scriptures. These other entries to the task of interpretation provide contexts, overviews, and perspectives that complement the book-by-book approach and discern dimensions of the Scriptures that the commentary design may not adequately explore.

The Bible as used in the Christian community is not only a collection of books but also itself a book that has a unity and coherence important to its meaning. Some volumes in this new series will deal with this canonical wholeness and seek to provide a wider context for the interpretation of individual books as well as a comprehensive theological perspective that reading single books does not provide.

Other volumes in the series examine particular texts, like the Ten Commandments, the Lord's Prayer, and the Sermon on the Mount, texts that have played such an important role in the faith and life of the Christian community that they constitute orienting foci for the understanding and use of Scripture.

A further concern of the series is to consider important and often difficult topics, addressed at many different places in the books of the canon, that are of recurrent interest and concern to the church in its dependence on Scripture for faith and life. So the series will include volumes dealing with such topics as eschatology, women, wealth, and violence.

The books of the Bible are constituted from a variety of kinds of literature such as narrative, laws, hymns and prayers, letters, parables, miracle stories. To recognize and discern the contribution and importance of all these different kinds of material enriches and enlightens the use of Scripture. Volumes in the series will provide help in the interpretation of Scripture's literary forms and genres.

The liturgy and practices of the gathered church are anchored in Scripture, as with the sacraments observed and the creeds recited. So another entry to the task of discerning the meaning and significance of biblical texts explored in this series is the relation between the liturgy of the church and the Scriptures.

Finally, there is certain ancient literature, such as the Apocrypha and the noncanonical gospels, that constitutes an important context to the interpretation of Scripture itself. Consequently, this series will provide volumes that offer guidance in understanding such writings and explore their significance for the interpretation of the Protestant canon.

The volumes in this second series of Interpretation deal with these important entries into the interpretation of the Bible. Together with the commentaries, they compose a library of resources for those who interpret Scripture as members of the community of faith. Each of them can be used independently for its own significant addition to the resources for the study of Scripture. But all of them intersect the commentaries in various ways and provide an important context for their use. The authors of these volumes are biblical scholars and theologians who are committed to the service of interpreting the Scriptures in and for the church. The editors and authors hope that the addition of this series to the commentaries will provide a major contribution to the vitality and richness of biblical interpretation in the church.

The Editors

PREFACE

It was only in the last year, already long past the publisher's due date, that I finally got going on this project. And once I did, I found that what started as a job of work, a project generated by another's desire, quickly became a work of love, a project driven by my own passion. The change in my own attitude occurred for at least four reasons.

First, I began to see how the topic of miracles is not one subject among others—as, say, the parables of Jesus—that can be restricted to the study of the biblical text alone; the issue of God's presence and power in creation is as real now as in Scripture. Second, miracles cannot be dealt with in a detached and dispassionate manner, for the mystery of God's presence and power inevitably involves us personally and demands a personal stance. Third, I saw more clearly that the question of miracles pervades the entire structure of Christian identity: we cannot engage the topic of the miraculous without taking on as well the central affirmations of the creed, such as the incarnation and the resurrection. Fourth, I realized more clearly that intellectual integrity demands taking on modernity's epistemological and cultural challenge to miracles, not least because many Christians today find their own faith compromised by a sort of double-mindedness.

This last point takes up all of part 1, "Framing the Discussion," and all of part 4, "Pastoral Implications." I spend all this time on the question of competing symbolic worlds because I am convinced that Christians have more or less given away the game by debating things like miracles in terms dictated by Enlightenment epistemology. Thus is the effort to demonstrate the possibility, probability, or reality of miracles by using historical methods. I argue, in contrast, that Christians need to recover singleness of vision by embracing a truly alternative vision of the world—not one that denies or dismisses the things that secular reason does well, but one that insists on the inherent and crippling limitations of secular reason in life's most important questions. That alternative vision, I show in chapter 3, involves imagining the world that Scripture imagines, recovering a proper and strong sense of creation, recognizing the validity of personal experience and narrative, and asserting the truth-telling quality of myth. The final chapter, in turn, suggests ways in which this project might affect the pastoral practices of teaching, preaching, prayer, and counseling.

Parts 2 and 3 of the book offer a way of thinking about the miracles of the Old and New Testaments. I do not attempt any defense of, or explanation for, specific signs and wonders. Instead, I offer an interpretation of miracles consonant with the biblical construction of reality that I argue in the other parts of the book. I hope that this approach will be of more benefit to Christians than the standard apologetic mode.

A word about the translation of scriptural texts. The default translation for the series in which this book appears is the New Revised Standard Version (NRSV). All my longer citations follow this version; a few follow the Revised Standard Version (RSV). In discussion, I sometimes cite more loosely, and occasionally I offer my own translation (AT = author's translation), based on the original language. In every instance, readers can consult the translations they use by means of the chapter and verse references.

Luke Timothy Johnson
Atlanta, Georgia
April 15, 2017

PART ONE

Framing the Discussion

CHAPTER 1

Miracles in Christian History

From the very first, Christians based their religious claims on the evidence provided by miracles—that is, experiences that could not be ascribed to merely human agency. They committed themselves to Christ, they said, because they experienced God's presence and power through Christ. In the Gospel of Luke (7:18–23), Jesus responds to John's question "Are you the one to come, or are we to wait for another?" with a list of wonders that support the claim that he is indeed the one: "The blind receive their sight, the lame walk, the lepers are cleansed, the deaf hear, the dead are raised, and the poor have good news brought to them" (Luke 7:22; see also Matt. 11:4–5). Peter declares to the crowd gathered at Pentecost concerning Jesus: "Jesus of Nazareth, a man attested to you by God with deeds of power, wonders, and signs that God did through him among you, as you yourselves know" (Acts 2:22).

The apostle Paul tells the Corinthians, "The signs of a true apostle were performed among you with utmost patience, signs and wonders and mighty works" (2 Cor. 12:12). He reminds the Galatians of the "miracles" the Spirit supplied among them (Gal. 3:5). He affirms to the Romans that his ministry among the Gentiles was carried out "by word and deed, by the power of signs and wonders, by the power of the Spirit of God" (Rom. 15:18–19). The Letter to the Hebrews similarly states that God has borne witness to the proclamation of the good news "by signs and wonders and

3

various miracles, and by gifts of the Holy Spirit, distributed according to his will" (Heb. 2:4).

The heart of the Christian message was, in turn, the greatest sign and wonder of all, the resurrection of Jesus and his exaltation to the right hand of God. That Jesus was the firstborn of the dead, raised by the power of God to become "life-giving spirit," was not simply one wonder among others, witnessed to by many believers (1 Cor. 15:1–11, 45): it was a reality experienced as well by those who were not witnesses to his appearances, but whose lives were being transformed by the power of God in the name of Jesus and through the Holy Spirit (2 Cor. 3:17). For believers, the resurrection experience was a "new creation" (Gal. 6:15; 2 Cor. 5:17) and the basis for a "new humanity" shaped in the image of Christ, who is the image of God (Col. 3:10; Eph. 2:15). The power of the Spirit deriving from the resurrected Lord was the source of all the other "miracles" (Gal. 3:5) worked among believers, including the gifts of glossolalia and prophecy (1 Cor. 12:4–11).

Such assertions concerning the immediate and present experience of God's power in the empirical realm—that is, among and within and through actual human bodies here and now—go together with a second bold claim: the messianic age proclaimed and celebrated by believers is in fulfillment of the prophecies contained in Scripture. The conviction is stated succinctly by 1 Peter 1:10–12:

> Concerning this salvation, the prophets who prophesied of the grace that was to be yours made careful search and inquiry, inquiring about the person or time that the Spirit of Christ within them indicated when it testified in advance to the sufferings destined for Christ and the subsequent glory. It was revealed to them that they were serving not themselves but you, in regard to the things that have now been announced to you through those who have brought you the good news by the Holy Spirit sent from heaven—things into which angels long to look!

In like manner, Paul declares that the proclamation of the gospel is the "revelation of the mystery that was kept secret for long ages but is now disclosed, and through the prophetic writings is made known to all the Gentiles" (Rom. 16:25–26). Indeed, the good news from God concerning his son was "promised beforehand through his prophets in the holy scriptures" (Rom. 1:2). The evangelists similarly take pains to show, as John puts it, that the Scriptures testify in Jesus' behalf (John 5:39). Mark is especially concerned to demonstrate that the beginning (Mark 1:1–3) and end (9:11; 14:21, 27) of Jesus' work is in fulfillment of what was written. Matthew aligns every aspect of Jesus' birth, ministry, and passion with specific passages in Scripture (e.g., Matt. 1:23; 3:3; 12:18–21; 13:13–15; 27:9–10). Luke has the risen Jesus himself connect his ministry, death, and resurrection to the writings of the prophets:

> "These are my words that I spoke to you while I was still with you—that everything written about me in the law of Moses, the prophets, and the psalms must be fulfilled." Then he opened their minds to understand the scriptures, and he said to them, "Thus it is written, that the Messiah is to suffer and to rise from the dead on the third day." (Luke 24:44–46)

Luke extends the fulfillment of prophecy to his account of the earliest church: among the things written, Jesus continues, are that "repentance and forgiveness of sins is to be proclaimed in his name to all nations, beginning from Jerusalem" (Luke 24:47). Throughout the narrative of Acts, the powerful presence of God among believers through "signs and wonders" is said to be in fulfillment of prophecy (e.g., Acts 1:15–20; 2:16–36; 3:23–26; 13:26–47; 15:10–17), even as his followers continue to interpret the story of Jesus as the fulfillment of prophecy (see 8:26–35).

Claiming the fulfillment of prophecy was, in its own way, as much an appeal to the miraculous as were assertions concerning healings and exorcisms. The prophets of old, after all, were thought to have spoken not on their own authority but through the impulse of the Holy Spirit—as clear an affirmation of God's present activity in the world as could be desired. Their utterances, in turn, were collected into writings that were themselves "spirit-inspired" (2 Tim. 3:16, *theopneustos*, AT). Finally, the experiences and events witnessed to by the first believers were, under God's control of history, a "fulfillment" of these ancient texts. The statement that Christ died and rose "according to the scriptures," then, is not a banal observation concerning literary concinnity, but a claim concerning God's presence and power in the empirical world (1 Cor. 15:3). For Christians throughout history, Scripture is no less an indication of

5

God's activity than are the "signs and wonders" of his continuing action among believers.

After the time of the New Testament, the experience of miracles continued to be celebrated by many, perhaps most, Christians. The second- and third-century apocryphal Acts of Peter and Thomas and John and Andrew feature signs and wonders even more spectacular than those found in the canonical Gospels. Similarly, apocryphal gospels like *The Protevangelium of James* and the *Infancy Gospel of Thomas* and *The Gospel of Peter* are replete with wondrous events. The writing of such compositions and their rapid dissemination through multiple translations over following centuries testify to the ready acceptance of the miraculous among believers.

By no means did believers consider the miraculous to be confined to the time of Jesus and the apostles. The power and presence of the living God continued to work in palpable fashion among the saints, those holy men and women who were understood in a mystical sense to be "other Christs" (Moss 2012). Miracles of various sorts, for example, were a standard feature of martyrologies, beginning already with the second-century *Martyrdom of Polycarp*, for the martyr above all was thought to be the one who perfectly realized conformity to the image of Christ: the power of God displayed itself in the triumph of the martyr's faith over death, just as the exaltation of Jesus with its outpouring of the Spirit on others vindicated the faithful death of Jesus. The celebration of the miracles worked through the martyrs—and the relics associated with them—is memorialized through the composition and reading of such collections as the *Martyrology of Usuard* (9th c.) and the authoritative *Roman Martyrology* (1583). The miraculous is also generously expressed in Christian art through the centuries (Jefferson 2014).

The evidence for God's continuing presence and power in the world continued to be displayed even after the age of persecution, among those whose lives could be regarded as conforming to the image of Christ. The *Lausiac History* of Palladius, for example, shows how miraculous deeds were attributed to the holy men and women who cultivated a radical discipleship in the wilderness. But even among those in a privileged social position, the wonders of God could be perceived to be at work. Thus Eusebius of Caesarea conceives of the pivotal career of Constantine in terms of "signs and wonders," from his vision of the cross at the Milvian Bridge, to his devout mother's finding the holy cross of Jesus in Jerusalem. The entire triumph of the Christian religion, its escape from persecution and establishment within the empire—however ambivalently later generations might regard it—was understandably perceived by those who experienced it as a miracle attributable to God alone (*Life of Constantine*).

Throughout the history of Christianity, ordinary believers considered the working of wonders as closely connected to sanctity: the presence and power of God was displayed above all through the bodies of those totally dedicated to God, not only during the life of the saint, but also (through relics) after their death. Thus, in his *Dialogues* (book 2), Gregory the Great (540–604) ascribed biblical-style miracles to the monastic founder Benedict of Nursia as a natural concomitant to his life of holiness. Growing collections of stories about the martyrs and other saints abounded in accounts of miracles, from Gregory of Tours's *Seven Books of Miracles* (6th c.) to the *Golden Legend* (1260)—the best-selling book of the Middle Ages, and to the *Roman Martyrology* (1583) and Alban Butler's *Lives of the Saints* (1756–59). Such a massive body of miraculous lore had been assembled by the seventeenth century that the Bollandist Society—a group of scholars dedicated to the study of the saints in order to distinguish the historical from the legendary—compiled the *Acta Sanctorum* in sixty-eight folio volumes, with publication of the first two volumes in 1643.

Despite the skepticism directed toward the miraculous by Enlightenment figures, as we shall see, a stout belief in the manifestations of God's presence and power within creation continued among Christians less influenced by the rationalistic premises of critics (Shaw 2006). The same enthusiastic embrace of the miraculous continues today, not only among Roman Catholics but also among many evangelical and Pentecostal Christians, and is shown by the many popular books devoted to the subject (Lewis 1947; Wakefield 1995; Metaxas 2014), as well as by the constantly proliferating sites on the Internet devoted to contemporary miracles associated with saints and places, such as Padre Pio, Lourdes, and Medjugorje (see, e.g., http://www.miraclesofthesaints.com/). Patterns of speech are also revealing. Many Christians continue to speak of miracles spontaneously and unself-consciously: "It was a miracle she was born healthy." "His escape from danger was miraculous." "We are praying for a miracle." "The disappearance of her cancer can only be called miraculous." In short, the majority of Christians have celebrated the presence and power of God in creation through signs and wonders, not only in the stories of the Old and New Testament, but also in their own lives.

Suspicion of Miracles

Other Christians, however, have regarded miracles with deep suspicion. They do not deny that signs and wonders can occur, but they question the source of such miracles or the religious value of them. This tendency begins with the attitude of Christian apologists toward the miracles claimed for pagan cults. The apologists regard such claims as deceptive, or worse, as the work of demons. Tatian (*Address to the Greeks* 18) and Justin (*1 Apology* 14) ascribe the revelations that people receive in dreams to demons; Tertullian (*Apology* 22–23) and Origen (*Against Celsus* 8.61) claim that the healings done at pagan shrines are doubly deceptive, because the demons both cause the illness and take it away; above all, prophetic revelation or divination is a sign of demonic power and deception (Tatian, *Address* 19; Tertullian, *Apology* 22–23; Origen, *Celsus* 4.89, 92).

The same sort of anxiety concerning the miraculous affects the apologists' attitude toward miracles claimed by Christians. Thus, although Justin's argument in his *Dialogue with Trypho* depends so heavily on the fulfillment of Old Testament prophecies, he pays little attention to the wonders performed by the ancient prophets and is suspicious of those claimed by recent prophets: Justin notes that "certain wonderful deeds" have been performed by false prophets to astonish people and "glorify the spirits and demons of error" (*Dialogue* 7). He declares that both true and false prophets did miracles (*Dialogue* 7) and concedes that the wondrous deeds worked by Jesus could be ascribed to magic (*1 Apology* 30). As for miracles performed in the present, he tends to attribute them to the work of demons who work through the rivals of the true Christian message, as in the miracles claimed for Simon, Menander, and Marcion (*1 Apology* 26, 56).

In sharp contrast to those writings (apocryphal gospels and acts, martyrologies) that celebrate the continuing power of God at work,

8

not only in Jesus but also through the risen Jesus in his apostles and other saints, the apologists of the second and third centuries are astonishingly reticent even concerning the wonders ascribed to Jesus in the canonical Gospels. Tatian, indeed, does not even mention Jesus in his apology (*To the Greeks*), presenting Christianity entirely in terms of its sane teaching about God, freedom, and the immortality of the soul. Similarly, Theophilus of Antioch makes only an oblique reference to the "voice of the Gospel" and makes no mention either of Jesus or of his wonders (*To Autolycus* 3.13–14). Athenagoras presents Christianity entirely in terms of its superior understanding of God and its moral instruction, referring to Jesus' teaching in Matthew and Luke, but without any reference to the wonders worked by Jesus (*Embassy* 4–12, 32–36). We find the same reticence concerning Jesus' wonders, along with silence concerning contemporary miracles, in the explicitly philosophical constructions of Christianity by Clement of Alexandria and Origen: for them, Jesus is above all the teacher whose words can transform, and the greatest miracle is the triumph of virtue over vice in the lives of transformed believers (see Clement, *Exhortation to the Greeks* 1.10–11; *Christ the Educator* 3.12; Origen, *Celsus* 1.67). For Origen, the healings reported of Jesus in the Gospels are continuous with the healing of believers' souls in the present (*Celsus* 1.67; 2.48).

How do we explain such a different perception of wonders than that found in popular Christian literature? The neglect of the miraculous among the early apologists, and the suspicion in which miracles are held, probably owes something to a specific religious disposition. In another study I have argued that Christianity inherited from Greco-Roman religion (and for that matter, also from Judaism) four distinct ways of being religious (Johnson 2009). The first way is participation in benefits: the divine power is seen as present and accessible in the empirical world, through a variety of phenomena, not least prophecies, ecstatic utterances, and miraculous deeds. The embrace of the miraculous by the Gospels and Acts—canonical as well as apocryphal—and by the majority of Christians through the centuries testifies to the continuing presence of this disposition.

The second way of being religious, however, is the way of moral transformation. Here the divine power may be acknowledged as active in empirical phenomena, but it is perceived as especially

9

operative in the minds and hearts of humans and is intended for their transformation. In this athletic form of religion, an emphasis on wonders "out there" may distract from the importance of change "in here" and lead to self-deception about what is religiously important. The third way of being religious is via transcending or fleeing the world; found among ancient Orphics and Christian gnostics, this way of being religious regards the entire visible world as deceptive precisely because it partakes in the material realm, which must be surpassed if the soul is to be saved. Among such spiritual adepts as well, the miraculous would be of little interest, above all when it involves a concern for materiality.

The second- and third-century apologists perfectly represent the second sort of religious disposition, found in the New Testament in the letters of Paul, James, and Hebrews. Right thinking and right acting is the point of religion and the proper expression of the divine power. Mature Christianity is not expressed so much by signs and wonders, as by the quiet moral change in humans and in the structures of human life. Insofar as the apologists and their successors defined themselves as philosophers and Christianity as the best of philosophies, they continued the tradition of such Greco-Roman moralists as Epictetus and Dio Chrysostom. We are not surprised, then, to find such writers suspicious of Christian wonders in the same way they were of pagan healings and prophecies, even attributing them in the same manner to demonic forces. The wonders may be real enough, but they can be deceptive or even destructive (Johnson 2009, 32–213).

Still other Christians were chronically suspicious of miracles. In Greco-Roman religion, a fourth way of being religious could be called "the way of stabilizing the world." For teachers like Plutarch, who was also a priest of Apollo at the famous prophetic shrine at Delphi, the most important expression of religion was the way in which it maintained "the city of gods and men" that constituted Greek civilization (Johnson 2009, 93–110). Christian bishops, many of whom were also monks and therefore committed to religion as moral transformation, carried on this concern for stability and security; thus many of them patrolled the borders of Christian identity by disputing with heretics and schismatics and by working to refine boundary-marking creeds (Johnson 2009, 234–54). They tended to resist claims to the miraculous because of what was perceived as their revolutionary and disruptive potential.

The case of speaking in tongues, or glossolalia—a gift of the Spirit that empowers humans to speech unavailable to them otherwise—illustrates the point. Although Irenaeus of Lyons has knowledge of the practice in churches, he excoriates the prophecy and ecstatic speech found among the followers of the Valentinian gnostic known as Marcus, whom Irenaeus regards as a charlatan and magician (*Against Heresies* 5.6.1; 1.14–16). Although forms of ecstatic utterance continued within some orthodox communities (see Origen, *Celsus* 7.9), it was progressively marginalized. By the beginning of the fifth century, bishops even professed ignorance of what Paul meant when he spoke of tongues in 1 Corinthians 14. John Chrysostom says, "This whole place is very obscure; but the obscurity is produced by our ignorance of the facts referred to and their cessation, being such as used to occur but no longer take place" (*Homilies on First Corinthians* 29, 32, 35). Similarly, Augustine of Hippo dismisses glossolalia as a special dispensation of the primitive church and of no pertinence to the church of his day (*Homilies on First John* 6.10; *On Baptism* 3.18).

The suspicion, if not the outright denial, of the miraculous continued among bishops and more philosophically inclined Christians through the following centuries. Claims to prophecy, ecstatic speech, or signs and wonders were consistently associated with doctrinal and moral deviance, requiring the authorities' most careful oversight. Such expressions of religion represent an unfortunate "enthusiasm" at odds with sober orthodoxy (see Knox 1950; Heyd 1995; Lim 2016), or as signs of a lapse into superstition (Lehner 2016, 125–53). Even within a Roman Catholicism that requires the proof of miracles by those who would be designated as saints, the hierarchy exercises an almost obsessive caution with respect to the demonstration of such wonders as "supernatural"; it tends to approach any freelance claim to the miraculous—be it Marian appearances at places like Lourdes and Fatima, or the claims to stigmata for such as Padre Pio or Therese Neumann—with the presumption of fraud or psychopathology.

Protestant Christians, in turn, are shaped by the bias of the early Reformation against miracles, not least the extraordinary gifts of prophecy and glossolalia, and tend to follow the position of Augustine: miracles were a distinctive manifestation of God's power during the period of the New Testament but are not to be credited today. The position that miracles ceased after the age of the

11

apostles (Cessationism) was argued most vigorously in the last century by the Princeton Reformed theologian Benjamin B. Warfield in his work *Counterfeit Miracles*. Warfield denied the authenticity of any but biblical miracles (1918, 5–6): "They represent the infusion of heathen modes of thought into the church" (61). But he spends so much energy discrediting the miraculous claims of the medieval and modern periods that he runs the risk of falling into a theologically perilous position. If God intervened in the time of the apostles through wondrous deeds, why should God not continue to do so in the life of the church through the ages? And if every claim to the miraculous in the life of the church can be dismissed as fraud or self-deception, does that not cast greater doubt on the miracles found in the New Testament? Restricting miracles to the Bible alone in effect reduces the living God of Israel to a *deus otiosus*, a god who may once have been active but now is removed, remote, and idle. It is a position that also stubbornly refuses to take seriously the witness of human experience through the ages.

Denial of Miracles

The systematic denial of the miraculous does not begin with modernity. The fourth-century-BCE philosopher Epicurus was not strictly an atheist in the modern sense: he did recognize a higher order of beings, "the blessed ones," whose happiness was directly correlated to their noninvolvement with the world (*Sovereign Maxims* 1). Epicurus sought to establish the same "freedom from disturbance" (*ataraxia*) among his followers by denying the reality of omens and portents and prophecies and by insisting that all phenomena can be explained by natural causes, rather than by appeal to divine powers. The first fear that Epicurus sought to banish was fear of the gods. His denial of the gods' involvement in the world is fundamental to his entire program: "If we had never been molested by alarms at celestial and atmospheric phenomena, nor by the misgiving that death somehow affects us, we should have had no need to study natural science" (*Sovereign Maxims* 11). Epicurus, in short, replaced the religious understanding of the gods as rewarding and punishing humans, teaching a vision of the world that excluded such external causality: the natural order is explicable on the basis of the accidental collision of atoms; the notion of a divine providence is

12

illusory. In ancient terms, Epicurus was thought to be an "atheist" precisely because he denied the presence and power of the divine among humans.

In his poem *On the Nature of Things* (*De rerum natura*), Epicurus's first-century-BCE disciple Lucretius celebrates poetically what he regards as the philosopher's liberation of humans from alienating religion: humans were "laying foully prostate upon earth crushed under the weight of religion," until the man from Greece stood up to religion and defeated it: "Religion is put under foot and trampled on in turn: us his victory brings level with heaven." Lucretius's poem provides samples of the natural science that displaces religion. Natural phenomena, above all the earthquakes, thunders and lightning that ordinary people thought to be divine portents, had completely natural causes (5.181–199). Providence was simply an empty notion (6.379–422).

The Epicurean attitude toward miraculous claims is applauded, in turn, by the brilliant second-century-CE satirist Lucian of Samosata. He reports how the Epicureans consistently resist the bogus religious claims of the charlatan Alexander of Abonoteichus, who started a cult of Asclepius in 150–170, based on elaborately rigged revelations (*Alexander the False Prophet* 25, 38, 44–45). Lucian displays the same attitude in his scathing portrait of the poseur philosopher Proteus Peregrinus (*The Passing of Peregrinus*, esp. 1–8, 42–45). Lucian's ideal philosopher, Demonax, displays a similarly distanced view of religion (*Demonax* 11, 23–24, 27, 34, 37), and in one of his more extravagant parodies, Lucian delights in recounting the absurd character of healings and prophecies and exorcisms (*The Lover of Lies* 16, 40).

Epicurus's denial of divine involvement with the world met with little approval in antiquity. His views were regarded as being destructive of the social order (see Epictetus, *Discourses* 1.23.1–10), and he was vigorously rebutted by Plutarch (*Is "Live in Obscurity" a Wise Precept?* [*Moralia* 1128B–1130E]; *Against Colotes* [*Mor.* 1107D–1127]; *A Pleasant Life Impossible* [*Mor.* 1086C–1107C]), who was a staunch defender of divine providence (*The Delays of the Divine Vengeance* [*Mor.* 548B–568]). Not until the European Enlightenment did a vigorous and principled denial of miracles again appear, now within a Christianity already shaped by the Reformation's rejection of all forms of catholic "superstition" (Johnson 2009, 10–12). Although the philosopher John Locke himself by no means rejected the notion of divine revelation (or the miracles of Jesus), his principle that revelation is to be judged by human reason speeds the way toward an interpretation of Christianity on purely rational terms (Locke 1695 = 2014). In his *Discourse of Miracles*, Locke says, "A miracle, then, I take to be a sensible operation, which, being above the comprehension of the spectator and in his opinion contrary to the ordinary course of nature, is taken by him to be divine" (Locke 1701 = 1823, 9:256–265).

But it was the British Deists of the seventeenth and eighteenth centuries who, under the rubric of "superstition," eliminated any trace of the supernatural from Christianity, including above all any claims to the miraculous. Works by John Toland (*Christianity Not Mysterious*, 1696) and William Wollaston (*The Religion of Nature Delineated*, 1724) argued that religion, including Christianity, must be measured solely by its reasonableness—with what is "reasonable" being measured in turn by the standards of an educated Englishman of the seventeenth century. The first British lives of Jesus followed suit, portraying Jesus as a purely human figure without any miraculous power (see Thomas Chubb, *The True Gospel of Jesus Christ*, 1739).

This background of a Christianity already defined almost entirely in rational terms provides the setting for the pivotal work of David Hume (1711–76), a Scottish thinker apparently devoid of any strong passion and having at best an attitude of superior condescension toward traditional Christianity. In the second edition of *An Enquiry concerning Human Understanding* (1751), Hume includes an argument concerning the possibility of miracles (or better, their nonpossibility) that he hoped would be "an everlasting check to all kinds of superstitious delusion, and consequently, will be useful as long as the world endures" (1.86). As the title to his work suggests, Hume's approach is not ontological ("do miracles happen?") but epistemological ("can we assent to the assertion that miracles happen?"). Humans can assent to something only if it is probable; probability in the case of human experience rests on the preponderance of evidence in favor of something happening. The essay concerns, then, the degree to which people should give an assent to claims of miraculous events (1.87–88).

14   Hume provides a definition of a miracle that he already turns, in the same sentence, to a denial of the miraculous: "*A miracle is a violation of the laws of nature*; and as a firm and unalterable

experience has established these laws, the proof against a miracle, from the very nature of the fact, is as entire as any argument from experience can possibly be imagined" (1.90). In a footnote, he offers an alternative definition: "A miracle may be accurately defined, *a transgression of a law of nature by a particular volition of the Deity, or by the interposition of some invisible agent*" (1.90; italics added).

Several aspects of his definition are at once noteworthy. First, the world of "nature" is conceived of as a closed system of cause and effect. Second, the "laws of nature" are known by humans because of their consistent experience; the "laws" therefore are deductions concerning reality that humans make based on experience (and experiment). Third, a miracle is defined in terms of a "violation"— or in his alternate definition, a "transgression" of these laws; the terms themselves are freighted with a negative nuance. Finally, in his alternative definition, the laws of nature are violated or transgressed by the "volition of the Deity" or the "interposition of some invisible agent."

Hume could, in fact, have defined a miracle in more neutral terms without altering his basic position. He could have spoken of an event that is the exception to ordinary human experience, or one that transcends ordinary human expectations (see Locke's definition above). Augustine, for example, had stated that "miracles do not happen in contradiction to nature, but in contradiction to what we know about nature" (*City of God* 21.8.2). By Hume's own account, the "laws of nature" are nothing more than the cumulative assessment of reality based on what people have already experienced. Moreover, since "the interposition of some invisible agent" necessarily maintains the invisibility of the agent, and since the "volition of the Deity" is likewise an inference from an experience rather than a fact verifiable by shared observation, Hume's entire discussion comes down to the weighing of human testimony: he pits the majority against the minority, the ordinary against the extraordinary.

On any matter of fact, Hume states, we correctly suspect witnesses who contradict each other, or are too few in number, or when they have a doubtful character, or when they have an interest in what they affirm, or when they are either hesitant in their assertions or too confident; these and other factors can "diminish or destroy the force of any argument, derived from human testimony" (1.89). But it is the sheer weight of "uniform experience" that counts most for Hume: "As a uniform experience amounts to a proof, there is

15

here a direct and full *proof*, from the nature of the fact, against the existence of any miracle; nor can such a proof be destroyed, or the miracle rendered credible, but by an opposite proof, which is superior" (1.90, emphasis original). Note here the slight but significant shift, from the credibility of witnesses concerning an event, to the existence of the event; it is not now for Hume whether we can reliably know about the miraculous, but that the miraculous does not exist at all.

Hume concludes his first section with a lengthy maxim, which sums up his position: "That no testimony is sufficient to establish a miracle, unless the testimony be of such a kind, that its falsehood would be more miraculous, than the fact which it endeavors to establish; and even in that case there is a mutual destruction of arguments, and the superior only gives us an assurance suitable to that degree of force, which remains after deducting the inferior" (1.91). He gives the pertinent example of someone claiming to have seen a dead man raised to life: the possibility that the person is either deceiving or being deceived convinces Hume to reject the claimed miracle; the pertinence of this rejection to classical Christian belief is obvious.

If in the first part of his essay Hume is able to maintain some degree of neutrality, his contempt for traditional belief in miracles is explicit in the second part, where he sets out four arguments against the probability of miracles. The arguments are not actually distinct but represent variations of the same theme: that which is ordinary in human experience is always to be preferred to that which is extraordinary. Hume first observes that there is no record in human history of witnesses so credible as to compel belief in the claim to miracles. Second, he states that witness to miracles is made suspect by the strong propensity of people to commit themselves to what is spectacular: they want to believe. Hume's tone reeks of contempt: "But what a Tully or a Demosthenes could scarcely effect over a Roman or Athenian audience, every *Capuchin*, every itinerant or stationary teacher can perform over the generality of mankind, and in a higher degree, by touching such gross and vulgar passions" (2.93, emphasis original).

His third argument is a simple variation of the first two: most accounts of miracles "chiefly abound among ignorant and barbarous nations" (2.94), or have been derived from such uneducated and credulous peoples. In this connection, Hume cites the example

16

of Alexander the false prophet, who was able to advance his religious scam precisely because he started it among ignorant and stupid Paphlagonians. He states, *"It is strange,* a judicious reader is apt to say upon the perusal of these wonderful historians, *that such prodigious events never happen in our days* (2.94, emphasis original). Hume's clear implication is that miracles are believed only among the ignorant of the past, and among the ignorant today; the educated person would never believe the stories that originated among such types and would never themselves claim to have experienced anything that could be called miraculous.

Hume's fourth argument is that all religions appealing to the miraculous as evidence for their faith claims cancel each other out. Because their teachings are contradictory, they cannot all be true, and the principle of contradiction applies to their claimed miracles as well. "This argument may appear over subtle [*sic*] and refined, but is not in reality different from the reasoning of a judge, who supposes that the credit of two witnesses, maintaining a crime against any one, is destroyed by the testimony of two others, who affirm him to have been two hundred leagues distant, at the same instant when the crime is said to have been committed" (2.95). He summarizes: "Upon the whole, then, it appears, that no testimony for any kind of miracle has ever amounted to a probability, much less to a proof; and that, even supposing it amounted to a proof, it would be opposed by another proof; derived from the very nature of the fact, which it would endeavour to establish" (2.98). In the end, the stable laws of nature trump any claim to a transgression of the laws of nature.

Hume ends his vigorous—but not nearly so logical as he supposes—treatment with a twofold dismissal of the miracles basic to the Christian tradition. First, all the miraculous events recounted in the Bible he regards as falsehoods (2.100). Second, he includes all claims to prophecy to have the same improbability as other miraculous claims (2.101). Hume's conclusion is that traditional Christianity is simply incompatible with the rationality celebrated by his peers of the late eighteenth century: "So that, upon the whole, we may conclude, that the *Christian Religion* not only was at first attended with miracles, but even at this day cannot be believed by any reasonable person without one" (2.101, emphasis original), by which, he means, that faith is itself a kind of miracle, contrary to reason.

17

The Enlightenment position finds one of its most sophisticated spokespersons in David Friedrich Strauss, whose *Life of Jesus Critically Examined* (first ed., 1835; 4th ed., 1860) was one of the pioneering efforts of what came to be called the historical-critical approach to the Bible, and whose specific approach to the miracle stories in the Gospels remains influential on later scholarly (and popular) efforts to interpret stories about the signs and wonders ascribed to Jesus. Strauss sought a middle ground between what he termed "supernaturalistic" interpretations of the miracles, which simply accepted them as real—the action of God active in Jesus—and "rationalistic" interpretations, which explained them away by reducing them to purely natural events (thus the feeding of the multitude is "explained" as the "miracle" of generosity stimulated by Jesus, by which everyone shared the food that they had brought).

Strauss advocated a "mythic" interpretation, not only of the explicit miracles, but also of the entire portrayal of Christ in the Gospels (1860, 33–76). Jesus is so clothed with the images attached to messianic expectations among Jews that it is extraordinarily difficult even to find a core of historicity in the Gospel accounts. Because the messiah was expected to work miracles, in short, those who believed in Jesus attributed miracles to him. In the long section of his work explicitly devoted to miracles, Strauss systematically examines each category of wonder (exorcism, healing, power over nature), dismissing in turn the rationalistic and supernaturalistic explanations before supplying his own mythical interpretation. It is possible, he states, that Jesus could have in fact "healed" a deranged person through his personal influence, but the entire realm of the divine and the demonic is mythic in character, so the picture of Jesus as introducing the rule of God by casting out demons cannot be regarded as properly historical, but as the interpretive work of believers employing the symbols of their age rather than our own (451–600).

Strauss's approach is brought to full realization in the twentieth-century work of Rudolf Bultmann, who applies "demythologization" not only to the miracles of Jesus, but also to the entire symbolic world of the New Testament. Readers in the twentieth century, he argues, cannot honestly affirm as true both the scientific explanation of the world, and the mythic construction of the world portrayed in Scripture (Bultmann 1941 = 1988); the task of the theologian is to

18

find within the New Testament the core of existential truth that lies covered over by mythic (that is, false) understandings of reality (Bultmann 1951–53).

Conclusion

As this brief survey has shown, miracles have been contested within Christianity from the beginning: while the majority of ordinary believers have gladly embraced the miraculous as the sign of God's presence and power among them, a significant minority of believers, especially those in leadership positions, have been chronically suspicious of miraculous claims.

Until recent centuries, however, such suspicion never rose to the level of a systematic denial of miracles. Suspicion might be attached to present-day claims to God's manifest presence and power, never to the miraculous events reported in Scripture. But under the influence of the European Enlightenment, a significant shift occurred. Now the denial of miracles along the lines of the ancient Epicurean critique is not repelled in the name of faith but is embraced as the sign of mature faith: in Deism and its continuing manifestations in mainstream Christianity, skepticism regarding miracles becomes the mark of an enlightened Christianity. A numerical majority of believers may continue to celebrate the miraculous past and present, but their witness is effectively marginalized by the dominant cultural order and by forms of Christianity that claim to speak for the tradition as a whole. The crisis of the present age is that the culturally most influential forms of Christianity have capitulated to a worldview that effectively eliminates the miraculous from serious consideration.

The reasons are not hard to discover. Rationalistic skepticism characterizes the classic historical-critical approach to the Old and New Testaments: academic engagement with miracle stories tends to be dismissive when it appears at all. In so-called historical Jesus research, the miracles ascribed to Jesus are regularly "bracketed" in favor of a portrayal of Jesus based on his sayings or on his prophetic (political) actions (Johnson 1996a). Such a reductionistic approach, in turn, is inculcated (sometimes flagrantly, sometimes subtly) in the study of the Bible in seminaries and schools of theology, in the name of "higher learning."

19

The formation of future ministers in such academic settings, in short, has become complicit in producing preachers of the good news who are embarrassed by talk of signs and wonders, and who (along with Hume) tend to regard claims to the miraculous as the sign of an ignorant and perhaps stupid population, a population that turns out to be, more often than not, the very people to whom ministers are called to preach. Symptomatic is the way the writings of the Episcopal bishop John Spong are taken by many "thoughtful Christians" as the only alternative to a dreaded "fundamentalism," even though his work is both derivative and puerile (Spong 1992, 1994).

Small wonder, then, that in congregations led by ministers formed in this fashion, claims to contemporary miracles are a cause of embarrassment rather than celebration, while sermons on biblical miracles become exercises in avoidance or interpretive sleight of hand. One of the central convictions of faith—traditionally, indeed, one of the bases for faith—has become, for the most educated and sophisticated of Christians, a deeply problematic category.

CHAPTER 2

The Problematic Category

The miraculous has at best become marginalized within most contemporary Christian discourse. To be sure, ordinary Christians, especially Pentecostals and Catholics, continue to speak among themselves about miracles, testify to the miracles done among them, and pray that signs and wonders be done for them and those they love. But believers who are ostensibly more evolved, those most affected by an Enlightenment construction of the world—among whom are probably at least some of the readers of this book—seldom think about miracles except perhaps as an unfortunate and slightly embarrassing reminder of premodern ways of seeing the world. Their avoidance of the topic implies that Christianity can do very well without claims to God's continuing presence and power in creation. But can it?

The forms of Christianity that have abandoned any consideration of the miraculous in the contemporary world find themselves in an even more difficult position with regard to the miracles reported in Scripture. The skeptic may ask, with David Hume, why do such signs and wonders happen only long ago and far away instead of in my neighborhood? But the Enlightenment believer who accepts Hume's argument is forced to the conclusion that those scriptural miracles are equally as impossible as the ones that they reject in contemporary reports. Thus the quest for the historical Jesus, as we have seen, begins with the premise that miraculous

21

deeds ascribed to Jesus and the apostles must be explained (that is, explained away) by appeal to misunderstanding, deception, fraud, or "mythologizing."

Such Christians, however, sometimes fail to reckon with the further and deeper implications of their rejection of God's continuing presence and power in creation, which touch on essential elements of the creed. With the explicit denial of the miraculous comes as well an implicit rejection of convictions for which centuries of believers lived and died—convictions concerning precisely extraordinary manifestations of God's presence and power (Johnson 2003).

If it is impossible for God's Word to be visibly present in the world today, for example, then neither can the Word have been made flesh in the person of Jesus, and any talk about the incarnation becomes nonsense (Hick 1977). If Jesus is not raised from the dead and exalted to God's right hand, to become the life-giving Spirit that transforms the lives of believers, then, as Paul declares, Christian faith is empty and hope of a future resurrection is foolish (1 Cor. 15:19). Note how directly Paul connects the general conviction concerning God's capacity to act in the world (the resurrection of the dead) with the specific claim as to how God acted in the world in Christ (his resurrection from the dead):

> Now if Christ is proclaimed as raised from the dead, how can some of you say there is no resurrection of the dead? If there is no resurrection of the dead, then Christ has not been raised; and if Christ has not been raised, then our proclamation has been in vain and your faith has been in vain. We are even found to be misrepresenting God, because we testified of God that he raised Christ—whom he did not raise if it is true that the dead are not raised. For if the dead are not raised, then Christ has not been raised. If Christ has not been raised, your faith is futile and you are still in your sins. Then those also who have died in Christ have perished. If for this life only we have hoped in Christ, we are of all people most to be pitied. (1 Cor. 15:12–19)

It was no accident that David Hume chose the example of a man raised from the dead as a claim that could not in any circumstances be believed, for he fully recognized how critical such a confession is for the classic form of Christianity. Without the robust confession of incarnation and resurrection, in turn, the expectation of a future

22

resurrection of the dead and of God's judgment of the living and the dead must be jettisoned as well. Logically, any authentic ground for the church's traditional understanding of the sacraments (above all baptism and the Eucharist) also disappears. If the sacraments are not means by which God's power works to change humans in the present, through the bodies and the bodily actions of believers, then they are nothing more than ritual acts that effect nothing more than a weak identity marker.

The forms of Christianity that suppress or deny the miraculous are consequently deracinated, cut off not only from the testimony of Scripture, but also from the creed and from centuries of living testimony given by the saints. Small wonder that Christianity so defined sometimes appears to be little more than a place for moral uplift and social improvement, lacking both a firm grasp on the good news of Scripture and a generous vision of God's power in the present. Having staked its future on a form of rationality that increasingly seems inadequate to life's genuine mysteries, such Christianity drifts, passionless and pointless, sustained mainly by institutional inertia and residual loyalty among its adherents. Before turning to some of the specific ways in which the miraculous is a problematic category for such Christians, it may be helpful to devote a little more attention to the reasons why the denial of the miraculous has taken such hold among them.

Marginalizing Miracles

The cleverness of David Hume was not by itself enough to secure such a widespread rejection of miraculous claims. His was only one of many voices passing the same judgment on miracles during the period we call the Enlightenment. Nearly a century before Hume, Baruch de Spinoza had already argued against the notion of miracles as exceptions to the "fixed and immutable order of nature" (Spinoza 1670 = 2001, 6.15–18) and considered those claiming miracles to be ignorant of the laws of nature (6.22). And after Hume, Immanuel Kant considered miracles as theoretically possible and acknowledged that they may have played a role in the founding of Christianity, but he thought that "sensible people do not warrant them in the affairs of life," declaring, "It is impossible for us to count on miracles or to take them into consideration in our use of

23

reason" (Kant 1793 = 1999, 2.2, "General Observations"). Three elements of Hume's discussion, however, have become standard. The first is his barely concealed contempt for those who believe in miracles. Only the ignorant or the befuddled can be gulled by miraculous claims; thus such claims do not occur among Hume's enlightened neighbors, only among those who lived in the dark ages or dwell in benighted lands. The second element is Hume's definition of miracles as having to do with individual acts in which an appeal to an unseen agency breaks or violates the established laws of nature. The third element is Hume's contention that such laws of nature are constant and universally acknowledged (by the knowledgeable), in contrast to the scattered witnesses claiming signs and wonders, whose credibility is always to be suspect precisely because their claims contradict how everyone knows the world works.

Hume's specific points are located, however, within a framework of understanding, broadly shared with other Enlightenment figures, that makes his arguments seem—to those within that framework—as self-evident. This construal of the world is best described as the secularization of consciousness (Johnson 2015, 64–85). Secularization reduces all reality to a self-contained and interlocking system of material causes and effects. Spirit is an unnecessary and therefore purely imaginary category. All that counts is what can be perceived by the senses. Science brings disciplined analysis to such material causes and effects and is therefore the privileged interpreter of the world thus construed. Just as "spirit" is less than real, so is "religion" displaced as a legitimate source of explanation for what happens in the real world. Science, allied with technology, is not only competent to explain the world understood completely in immanent terms, but also capable of changing it.

The success of science and technology through such a reduction to the material has been remarkable and is the strongest argument possible that just such a reduction, together with the hegemony of scientific inquiry, is necessary for human progress. It is impossible to argue against the techniques of measurement and manipulation when their practitioners can point not only to conquests over sickness and disease, but also to breaking genetic code of human life itself; when they can claim to have improved the "standard of life" for millions around the world; when they can point to journeys to outer space and explorations to the ocean's depths; when all the earth's populations are increasingly forming a global village through electronic communication.

Compared to such positive accomplishments, the use of technology for genocide, the persistence of poverty, ecological damage, the pestilence of narcotics addiction among the earth's most advanced populations—all these can be dismissed by the committed secularist as a failure to have been sufficiently rigorous in the use of scientific methods, or even the fault of lingering superstition. For the secularist, the world holds no mysteries, only sets of problems and solutions. The problems that remain simply need better solutions, and science is uniquely equipped to discover them. In a fascinating historical turn, the most rabid ideologues of secularity tend to regard those who continue to appeal to divine causality in the same way that ancient heresiologists regarded those who contradicted the church's creed: they are outliers whose stubborn adherence to an erroneous worldview is responsible for hindering human progress.

The secular perspective and the success of technology, within its carefully circumscribed arena of activity, have together succeeded in creating what Mircea Eliade presciently called a "hominized" consciousness, in which people are seldom in direct contact with God's creation and interact almost totally within structures and systems constructed by humans themselves (Eliade 1959, 204). In the cybernetic revolution, human brain circuits and the electronic circuits of machines form a "virtual reality" that is so appealing, so convincing, that it can be mistaken for reality as such and can indeed be engaged as simply what is real.

Secularism today is not merely one among other ideologies: it is the dominant ethos of what we call the First World—those people, wherever they live, who are most shaped by the marriage of Enlightenment reason and technology and are most contemptuous of magic, mystery, and miracles. Nowhere are the assumptions of an aggressive secularism more evident than among those representing "the New Atheism," the titles of whose books communicate effectively their contemptuous stance toward all religion, yet above all, Christianity: *God Is Not Great: How Religion Poisons Everything* (Hitchens 2007); *The God Delusion* (Dawkins 2006); *The End of Faith: Religion, Terror, and the Future of Reason* (Harris 2004); *God: The Most Unpleasant Character in All Fiction* (Barber 2016).

But the evidence for the secularization of culture is all around us: in the decline of traditional religious practice and discourse, especially in the public sphere; in the premises governing entertainment, commerce, and politics—the three realms are sometimes scarcely distinguishable; and in the rules for respectable argumentation set by the academy, which is perhaps most forceful in potentiating the influence of the secular disposition through the indoctrination of the young. And precisely the degree to which the standards of the secular world (thus construed) have infiltrated the church, Christians find themselves in a condition of cognitive dissonance when it comes to miracles. From one side, they are pressed by the claims of Scripture and tradition concerning the work of the living God in the world; from every other side, they are pressed even more powerfully by the cultural assumptions of the world in which they live, assumptions that make the miraculous a problematic category.

Consequences of Double-Mindedness

The Letter of James warns readers against "double-mindedness" (Jas. 1:8; 4:8), by which the author means trying to live by two opposing measures simultaneously. His readers want to profess the faith "in our glorious Lord Jesus Christ" (2:1), but at the same time they act in accordance with values of "the world" that are contrary to that faith. James emphatically asserts that they cannot maintain "friendship with the world" and be friends "with God" (4:4): they must live consistently by one standard or the other (Johnson 1985). James has in mind the opposition between a view of the world (the wisdom from above) that is open to God's creation—and therefore logically leads to practices of gift-giving, hospitality, and mutual assistance in a community of collaboration—and a view of the world (the wisdom from below) that sees the world as a closed system, which logically leads to practices of envy, competition, oppression, war, and even murder. When the Christian community claims to live God's measure but lives in a fashion that contradicts that measure, then the Christian community is in serious need of conversion to simplicity and purity of heart.

26

Contemporary Christians infected with the spirit of the Enlightenment regarding miracles find themselves, I think, in an analogous form of double-mindedness, caught in the tension between the claims of the tradition and the demands of modernity. The most obvious example is revealed in the quest for the historical Jesus that was launched in the eighteenth century precisely as Enlightenment's effort to displace the Christ of dogma, and that has become, in the early twenty-first century, the badge of an intellectually sophisticated form of Christology among the best-educated Christian congregations.

In worship, such Christians address Jesus as risen Lord and pray to God the Father through him; they hear readings from the apostle Paul that speak of Jesus as Lord, and readings from the Gospels that speak of Jesus as Son of God and describe his wondrous acts of healing and exorcism; they may share a Eucharist that declares of the bread given to each of the faithful, "the body of Christ." In short, the forms of worship are drenched with convictions concerning Jesus as "true God of true God," the one through whom the living God disclosed himself in the past, and—here is the point—*continues* to disclose himself in the present through the medium of the Holy Spirit active in the worship of the congregation.

But in Sunday school classes after worship, or in the Adult Forum classes featuring visiting scholars, this Jesus disappears and is replaced by a variety of historically reconstructed Jesus figures: now a prophetic reformer, now a Cynic preacher, now a revolutionary, now a mystic—but always, a Jesus considered quite apart from, if not always explicitly opposed to, the Jesus confessed by the creed (Johnson 1999a). Worship is shaped by the Jesus of the Gospels, who works wonders and whose entire presence is a revelation of God's power in the world; adult study focuses on a Jesus abstracted from the Gospels, especially through avoidance of the topic of Jesus' miracles.

The dissonance is seldom made explicit. Many experience worship, after all, as a time of consolation rather than challenge; they wake up their minds only in time for adult education. More energy than is ordinarily available to elderly Presbyterians or Methodists is required to awake the conflict between the Christ who is source of salvation in worship and the Jesus who is the subject of historical analysis in the schoolroom. But the dissonance is certainly present implicitly and even surfaces, as I will show shortly, in preaching.   27

The working Enlightenment definition of a miracle as the breaking of the established laws of nature by a divine agency has also engendered double-mindedness concerning classic philosophical and theological questions among contemporary Christians. How should we think generally, for example, about the relation of the divine to the visible world? On one side is the biblical portrayal of the living God, who is active in creation in diverse ways, displaying his presence through acts of power. On the other side is the conception of the world, derived ultimately from the Epicureans and propagated primarily by Deists, as a self-enclosed system of natural laws that may have been put in motion by a divine agency, but now runs independently and on its own terms. On one side "creation" is an ongoing process dependent at every moment on God; on the other side "nature" is a totally independent process driven by immanent and not transcendent causes. It is obvious that the Humean definition pits these understandings against each other and insists that the Epicurean option must obtain—for the "laws of nature" are accessible to all and universally agreed upon, whereas the "acts of God" are based on individual testimony and contradicted by universal experience.

Once more, the contemporary Christian engages the biblical conception of the living God in worship on Sunday morning, but lives within the secular conception of nature in daily life, a conception reinforced powerfully by the machinery of cultural formation (entertainment, politics, education). One way of dealing with the dissonance, to be sure, is simply shutting the two conceptions into separate compartments of the mind, corresponding to the two cultural settings. On Sunday, we pray for God to save us; on Monday through Saturday, we act as though salvation is entirely up to us. Another option is to capitulate completely to the Epicurean option: the empirical world is an independent reality with its own rules and must be dealt with on its own terms; in that secular universe, an appeal to God's intervention in the form of miracles interjects superstition into the realm of pure rationality.

By jettisoning the possibility of God acting through signs and wonders, however, another central conviction of all traditional believers is put in jeopardy: the belief that God directs human events to God's own ends for his creation. This is the doctrine of divine providence. God not only brings the world into existence; God also sustains it in existence and directs it to a telos that is God's own. The doctrine requires that "nature" not be independent of the divine action—as construed by modernity—but precisely as

28

creation be deeply responsive to the divine will. This theological conviction concerning God's providence, in turn, traditionally
involves the belief that God is judge of all creatures, above all the
judge of human actions, and that God rewards the good and pun-
ishes the wicked. At the heart of this belief is not a theory of how
God judges—as in various end-time scenarios—but rather that, as
creator, God has maker's knowledge of his creatures and discerns
hearts righteously (Johnson 1990a, 20–23). But if God is incapable
of acting in the small things of quotidian existence, the realm of
what is often thought of as the "miraculous," then God is certainly
incapable of directing the world to its appointed end or of judging
the deeds of humans.

Christians who cling to the traditional convictions concerning
providence and God's judgment, while at the same time accepting
the Humean definition of the miraculous, however, also struggle
with the questions of theodicy identified already in Scripture (see
Pss. 10:1–18; 113:1–6; 22:1–31; 53:1–6; 73:1–28): if God is in charge
of reward and punishment, why do the righteous suffer and the evil
prosper? Or, with respect to miraculous interventions, why should
God reach out to heal this person and not that one? Why should this
affliction receive divine attention and not that affliction? At issue
here is not only the fact of God's capacity, but also of God's fairness.
Thus the events of the Holocaust, in which millions of Jews were
slaughtered simply because they were Jews, pressed these questions with distinctive urgency: if God does not intervene to rescue
innocent people whose very existence as a people is threatened
with extinction, thoughtful persons can conclude that God either
is truly powerless to act within human affairs, or that God is in fact
not a righteous God who keeps his promise to those who serve him
(see, e.g., Rubenstein 1992; Fackenheim 1991).

The most recent effort to address these tensions has been
made by liberation theology, which preserves convictions concerning God's righteousness by reducing convictions concerning God's
transcendent power. God sides with the poor and oppressed but
lacks the ability to assist them through miraculous interventions.
Instead, God identifies with those movements of human liberation
that seek to do justice in the world. Liberation theology is a mix
of process and political theologies: God does not stand above and
apart from creation as its cause and sustainer, but God is in the process of becoming together with an evolving world. God's presence

29

in the world is precisely through human agents working to reverse oppression and injustice through social systems that enhance the humanity of all.

The attractive feature of liberation theology is its passion for social justice and its desire to maintain a link with the living God of Scripture, who sides with the poor and oppressed. But this positive gain is won by identifying the divine presence with human idealism and social engagement (L. Boff and C. Boff 1987; Cone 1970; Williams 2013). The only miracles are those of social change, accomplished through hard and united human effort. In a very real sense, liberation theology represents an almost complete capitulation to the spirit of modernity, simply replacing its cool rationality with social passion.

The secular perspective of modernity makes Christians double-minded with respect to fundamental aspects of classic Christian tradition, including Christology, creation, providence, and eschatology. Christians' unease about miracles is part of this divided consciousness: secularity's ethos prevents a wholehearted embrace of the miraculous, cutting them off from the witness of Scripture and from the largest part of the tradition.

That such double-mindedness is not simply theoretical is revealed by uncertainty and inconsistency in pastoral practice. Pastors whose theological education paid no attention to miracles find themselves singularly unprepared for some situations of care and counseling. Nostrums about the political program of the historical Jesus, or humanity's hope for a liberated future, have little applicability when a child lies desperately ill, or a spouse is caught in self-destructive addictions, or a father learns that he faces early senility, or a young wife despairs at another unsought pregnancy. In such existential crises, both the content and character of faith is tested. What is it that we believe? How coherent is the structure of our belief?

A pastor who is uncomfortable with the proposition that, by the incarnation, God has chosen to participate forever in our suffering, or with the conviction that the death and resurrection of Jesus enables our suffering to be caught up in the victory of God over sin and death, or with the thought that fervent prayer to God for his saving intervention even or especially when every human possibility seems to have been foreclosed—that pastor can have little helpful to say in such situations. If the minister has been trained to

30

regard talk about faith healing as silly, or language about miracles as superstitious, the minister is rightly perceived as bringing little to such human crises beyond what Methodist piety terms a "non-anxious presence." If anyone puts the questions "Is it legitimate to pray for a miracle here and now, for God to turn this around? Is such prayer an expression of authentic faith or a distortion of it?," the minister ought to be able to answer simply and directly in the affirmative. But such a simple stance is difficult for ministers trained in schools that have excised miracles from their theological lexicon.

It is in preaching, above all, that ministers' double-mindedness is most exposed. The preachers stand before the assembled faithful as witnesses to the truth of the Scripture as it is read in worship. Yet the preachers' capacity to bear such witness is hobbled by the cultural outlook that not only affects their own view of reality, but also has deeply affected the theological education that was intended to prepare them to preach. Here is a case in which passages from the Gospels that probably seemed most meaningful to their first readers—because they demonstrated how the power they experienced as coming from the risen Lord was active as well in the ministry of Jesus—are avoided when possible, or explained away when engagement is unavoidable. It is in the preacher's unease and embarrassment that the destructive consequences of partially digested historical-critical knowledge emerge into full view. Preachers, after learning Scripture from biblical scholars whose only epistemological lens is historical, find that they have little to say about miracles when forced to preach on them.

The epistemological lens of faith, in contrast, enables other forms of engagement with Scripture. The stories of Jesus' healings and exorcisms, for example, provide the opportunity to inquire into the forms of healing and liberation from captivity now being experienced in the church—or the lack of such healing and liberation, against which the church should prophesy. If such contemporary signs and wonders have been ruled out of account because miracles do not happen, then the Gospel accounts are reduced to implausible fables from ancient and unenlightened people.

The miracle stories of the Gospels are not alone in suffering such neglect and diminishment. The entire range of language in Paul's Letters having to do with religious experience—how human lives are being transformed by the power of God in the here and

31

now—is ignored, as the preacher reaches for the more manageable registers of doctrine or ethics. But Paul's language about religious experience obviously invites the preacher to examine the ways in which the church in the here and now might also be experiencing (or lacking in the experience of) the transforming power of the Holy Spirit in everyday lives. Paul's language about the experience of the Holy Spirit provides a guide for an examination of the congregation's own life. But if the pastor is deaf to religious experience in the present and has no ear for forms of ecstatic speech, prophecy, and healings among the people, then Paul's language seems without point. The lack of an experiential correlative in the present encourages avoidance of experiential language in the texts of Scripture.

The way to a singleness of vision will be difficult, but it can be prepared for by a preliminary consideration of some of the deeply problematic aspects of the dominant cultural construal. In the next chapter I will propose a positive alternative through imagining the world that Scripture imagines—an approach that enables a robust appreciation of the presence and power of God in today's world, and an opening to a deeper appreciation of the accounts of signs and wonders in the Bible. To conclude the present chapter, I simply identify some intrinsic weaknesses in the construal of the world that dictates the rejection of miracles by nonbelievers and also by many "sophisticated" Christians.

Weaknesses in the Dominant Position

At least four weaknesses in the secular position concerning miracles can, if taken seriously, go some way toward shaking the confidence with which many people embrace it.

Laws of Nature

Spinoza and Hume and many after them speak of the "immutable" laws of nature that miracles must violate through a divine intervention. The phrasing makes it sound as though the laws were mechanistically wired into the very processes of the material world as an immanent element in the processes themselves. For Deist thinkers, these "laws of nature" are the expression of a divine ordering, which not even God can interrupt without betraying God's original design.

32

In fact, however, the concept "law of nature" is much more elusive than it at first appears. The "law," as Chesterton once observed, is not really that of "nature"—itself a human conceptualization rather than something simply given—but of the human mind as it observes the world and develops certain principles and axioms: "all the terms used in the science books, 'law,' 'necessity,' 'order,' 'tendency,' and so on, are really unintellectual, because they assume an inner synthesis, which we do not possess" (Chesterton 1908 = 1959, 53). They are not laws to which nature must bend, but rather consistent patterns of occurrence that humans have so far been able to notice and record. For the sake of simplicity, to be sure, it does no harm of speak of the "laws of nature" as tentative and operative human hypotheses concerning the material order, so long as an inappropriate projection of human cognition onto the processes themselves is avoided. The notion that God is constrained to act in accordance with human observations concerning ordinary patterns of occurrence is, once one thinks about it, ludicrous, as is the precipitous and arrogant conclusion that an event outside the ordinarily observed pattern of occurrence is a "violation" of a pattern that exists only in the order of human cognition, not in the things observed.

Contrary to Hume's opposition between the immutable laws of nature and the subjective claim to the experience of miracles, furthermore, the construction of hypotheses, principles, and axioms also depends on subjective human experience. There are cases, to be sure, when scientific method gives a greater sense of neutrality and objectivity to such observation, especially when mechanical means of perception, measurement, and manipulation are employed. But even in these cases, it comes down to what is observed and what is recorded by a human subject. The Enlightenment assumption that a nonsuperstitious view of the world would yield a universal and stable consensus concerning natural processes is neither self-evident nor supported by actual experience. The interpretation of material phenomena is not unaffected by social class and other cultural factors. At the level of human testimony, there is no real difference between one person's claim to have experienced healing, another's claim to have experienced sexual abuse, another's claim to have experienced a concentration camp, and another's claim to have seen a solar explosion through a telescope; nor is any one of these claims, at the level of human testimony, any more or less plausible than the others.

33

The human capacity to postulate "laws" concerning material processes, furthermore, varies widely. Even in the very best cases, it is partial. To put it as bluntly as possible, even in the early twenty-first century—leaving aside the relative "dark ages" of David Hume and Benjamin Franklin—human knowledge of the material world is far from sufficient, much less complete. The situation is much better in some areas than in others: mathematics and physics are outstanding examples of steady and impressive growth in knowledge, as are the fields of geography and geology. But the closer we get to the properly human, the more uncertain are the supposed "laws." Even with the amazing breakthrough in biology represented by the discovery of DNA and the multiple theoretical and practical advances in that area, however, a great deal about the human organism remains obscure and maddeningly elusive. One can simply catalog the ever-changing theories on something so basic as human nutrition over recent decades to see how uncertain are "the laws" of nutrition.

And if we turn to psychology, the rise and fall of entire schools of psychology in the last hundred years suggests that a comprehensive understanding of the human psyche has not yet been attained. To be sure, those who have reduced psychology to brain chemistry can claim to have mastered human behavior through medical manipulation, but quite apart from the change of subject this involves—we have failed to understand or heal the psyche, so let's pretend it does not exist—the sad and often tragic consequences of chemical (and surgical) manipulation of humans is well attested. The notorious scientific "softness" of those fields called the social sciences (sociology, anthropology, economics, political science), in turn, supports the proposition that the capacity of humans to determine the "laws of nature" is indeed meager.

A final example of how the supposedly "immutable laws of nature" postulated by Hume and Spinoza are actually sets of hypotheses drawn from human observation is the way in which such hypotheses change over the course of time. Certainly, such change is appropriate and inevitable if we are talking, not about qualities inherent to material properties, but about assessments of behavior patterns in such properties carried out by humans: further and better observations ought to lead to fuller and better hypotheses. But this natural scientific process is something far more fragile and uncertain than the unalterable laws that miracles are thought to disrupt.

34

The assumption that "everyone knows" this or that on the basis of "scientific consensus," furthermore, is repeatedly disconfirmed by the history of science and sometimes by cultural history. Those who shared with David Hume the comforting thought that eighteenth-century Europe represented the best realization of human civilization were certain that the populations of Africa, Asia, and even the Americas were inferior in character and probably in "nature." Similarly, in the nineteenth century, under the rubric of natural science (supported by such "objective" techniques as physiognomic profiles and phrenology) "laws" concerning racial superiority were rampant and enjoyed remarkably widespread acceptance. Indeed, within the past century, the best scientific minds in Europe and America were persuaded that eugenics—involving birth control, sterilization, and forced abortions among those of undesirable racial characteristics—would shortly lead to a superior humanity. Likewise, the most enlightened and informed minds were certain that capitalism and nationalism were destined to disappear within a short period of time because of the "inexorable laws" of dialectical materialism. Or, to take a contemporary example, just as "everyone now knows" on the basis of scientific consensus that climate change is leading inexorably to a global warming that will be catastrophic for human society, so in the 1970s, based on the best scientific analysis, "everyone knew" that an equally apocalyptic future of global cooling was bound to occur.

Individual Act

A second major deficiency in the default definition of a miracle is its focus on a singular act or event. To some extent, the binary opposition between miracle and nonmiracle is established by believers themselves. They point to something that has or is happening as a *thauma*, a cause for wonder, and they praise God for the *sēmeion*, sign of God's presence and power. When they point to some occurrences as signs and wonders and not to others, however, the implication can be drawn that those not so identified are not the work of God in the same way. Such a distinction between different acts and events invites disputation concerning God's activity: if God is claimed to be directly at work in this action, does that mean God was absent from this other action? Or was God passively present in one event and actively present in the other? Attention paid to

35

separate discrete acts inevitably leads to proving or disproving that they "violate the immutable laws of nature" and therefore can legitimately be called a miracle. The focus shifts from "the wonder" of the event to the cause of the event: was it divine agency or mere nature working itself out?

The problem of thus isolating discrete events or actions is two-fold. First, even as it draws attention to efficient causality (what did this?) rather than the wondrous character of the event (we did not expect this), it oversimplifies the issue of causality itself by casting it in terms of an either/or: either this healing occurred through a word of prayer, or it is due to the application of medicine. We recognize how these might on occasion be mutually excluding: we were in the wilderness with no medicine and had only prayer (and suddenly he got better); or, the medicine was injected without any of us being aware of it (and suddenly the fever left). But these are usually false alternatives: God can be at work in the antibiotic (and all the science that enabled it to be placed in the body), and the antibiotic can be sped on its work through the prayer of faith.

The causes and occasions of both illness and recovery are infinitely complex. Emotional and spiritual dispositions can be a major factor in both psychological and somatic disease, just as chemical imbalance can contribute both to organic and psychological distress. Conversely, the power of prayer, faith, hope, and love in the process of healing cannot be denied, any more than can the power of vitamins, exercise, and inhalants. The fact that multiple causes are at work neither adds to nor subtracts from the "wonder" character of a healing. Nor can it be stated that God is more clearly at work in prayer than in a timely injection.

An excessive focus on individual acts can also have the effect of obscuring the fact that a *thauma* or *sēmeion* can be disclosed through a long period of time or series of events. Is healing less impressive, for example, when it takes place over a long period of recuperation and rehabilitation? Is it any less a *thauma*, when the expected outcome was not healing but destruction? Deathbed recoveries, like deathbed conversions, are undoubtedly dramatic. But they are no more significant as a sign of God's presence and power than a slow process of conversion that takes place over many years.

36   Similarly, concentration on individual acts leads to a failure to appreciate the *thauma* that can be revealed through long-range and complex social processes. A pertinent example is the "sign and

wonder" that was the Declaration on Religious Freedom issued by the Second Vatican Council (*Dignitatis Humanae*, 1965). Nothing in prior Roman Catholic polity or practice could have led anyone to anticipate such an emancipatory statement concerning the rights of the individual conscience and the freedom of individuals to practice their faith without interference from state or church. Indeed, the dominant position in Catholicism was that "error has no rights," and efforts by ecclesiastical authorities to suppress what was termed "heresy" were common, not least as it was thought to occur among clergy and theologians. Some European theologians continued to argue up to the very eve of the council that religious freedom was no real right (Johnson 1996b).

So, how did such a remarkable and unexpected turnabout take place? Primarily through the diligent theological effort of a single American Jesuit, John Courtney Murray, who throughout a decades-long career as a scholar wrote and spoke on the benefits of the American experience of separating church and state (see Murray 1960). Murray's work, in fact, had itself come under Vatican suspicion and censure. But at the Council, his work was taken up by the gathered bishops and provided the basis for a declaration on religious freedom that no one knowing previous Catholic history could ever have predicted. It was truly something new, something unaccountable on the basis of ordinary politics, something that profoundly changed the course of the church on a matter of the most profound importance, and it constituted what, in my view, can properly be called a miracle: a disclosure of God's presence and power in a manner and degree irreducible to the ordinary expectations for human activity.

The Concept of Nature

The final two weaknesses in the conventional framing of miracles will be addressed more fully in the next chapter but can be stated succinctly here. I addressed the question of "immutable laws of nature" above, suggesting that greater precision and humility ought to accompany such language. But it is important to note as well that the entire construction of "nature" as something standing apart from, and independent of, both God and humans is questionable. Far from being something self-evident and simply given, as such "laws" seemed to imply, nature as used by Enlightenment thinkers

37

is a concept that is constructed on the basis of distinct premises that are by no means self-evident.

In this construction, the empirical world available to the senses is a self-contained system of causes and effects, an interconnected series of mechanical arrangements that are observable and measurable. In this sense nature is, by definition, distinct from the divine, except through the way in which the internally coherent system was set in place through a remotely prior divine activity and then left on its own. But it is also distinct from the properly human. Except as it is an object of study and analysis (and perhaps manipulation), the realm of nature does not embrace human experience and behavior. In this view, humans are observers of nature, not part of nature.

The growth of knowledge over the past centuries has revealed what a narrow and insufficient view of the empirical world was available to thinkers like David Hume, and how untenable was their construction of nature. Above all, the picture of humans standing apart from nature as outside observers has been shown to be fundamentally flawed. Two scientific advances in particular have shaken Enlightenment premises concerning humans as privileged observers. The first is the understanding that humans have evolved together with other species as part of an overarching process of natural selection. Darwin is often properly thought to have challenged traditional Christian faith, and so he did; but no less did his theory—and its subsequent development into one of the dominant explanatory frameworks for the world—shake up the complacent assumptions of the Enlightenment concerning the special place of humans (McGrath 2015).

Since European males share most of their genes with the primates and appear to have emerged from among such primates with some distinctive qualities, two corollaries emerge: first, European males are very much a part of rather than set apart from natural processes; second, the precise "causes and effects" by which humans emerged as distinctive do not appear as the working out of an inexorable law with a predictable outcome, but have a definite air of chance or happenstance about them. Evolutionary psychology pushes the link between humans and other animals even further: in a manner virtually identical to other mammals, the "selfish genes" within humans dictate fundamental choices (such as choice of mate) at a level inaccessible to the cool rationality thought to be essential to the enlightened European male.

The development of ecological science has made even clearer the physical interconnections, not simply between humans and other mammals, but also among humans and all the rest of the material world, alerting us to the fact that we do not stand outside "nature" as observers but exist very much within the empirical world as participants. Humans not only work on the world, the world also works on humans; the human animal is a microcosm of the larger ecology in which it participates. The process of exchange among organisms is infinitely complex and interdependent. Microbes do not simply enter the body from the outside: they are already inside the human body, doing their quiet work. People not only consume the earth: as they exhale and eliminate, they also renew the earth. Just as disruption in the conditions of organic survival threatens human existence, so can human misuse of material resources threaten to destroy the conditions of organic survival. Humans do not stand apart from but firmly within an ecosystem that includes all other living beings—as well as the elements of earth, water, and air that make organic life possible.

Developments in theoretical physics, along with discoveries in astrophysics and geophysics, have likewise shattered the Enlightenment image of nature as a well-ordered and self-contained system, whose workings could best be compared to those of a clock (Maitland 1995). The universe now seems wilder and more unpredictable by far. The world is not a finished product but an ongoing process: the universe expands and discloses to its observers impenetrable mysteries like antimatter and black holes; the earth's tectonic plates constantly shift, altering as they move the depths of the sea and the surface of the planet; volcanic eruptions generated by such seismic shifts create new landscapes and effect climate changes. Einstein's theory of relativity showed the limited applicability of the Newtonian physics thought to be "unalterable" by the savants of the eighteenth century, and his theory changed our fundamental conceptions of time and space. And the quantum physics of Nils Bohr made us aware of an element of indeterminacy, even of chance, among subatomic particles. In short, the world now seems more open, fluid, unpredictable, and even random than it did to David Hume and his friends.

An expanded awareness of the world's potential to surprise and shock has come about as well through greater exposure to a wider range of human experience than was available to the enlightened gentlemen of eighteenth-century England, who thought they had

39

seen everything but had actually seen comparatively little. Take, for example, the kinds of religious experiences that Hume and his fellows dismissed as deriving from a superstition that exposed a lack of education, or as a form of "enthusiasm" exposing mental illness. But even among the highly educated, as Sigmund Freud showed, dreams can indeed be revelatory, if not of transcendent realities, then of the deep immanent forces at work in the human psyche. Visions have come to be regarded as providing distinctive insight into the present structure of reality (as in Einstein's "vision" of moving trains), or a prophetic insight into the future shape of society (as in Martin Luther King's "I Have a Dream" speech). Social scientific studies have shown, in turn, that glossolalia, while sometimes involving a form of psychological dissociation, can be positively correlated to mental health (Malony and Lovekin 1985; Hine 1965).

What about experiences that are not specifically religious? Medical practice is constantly chastened by experiences of healing that seem to have little to do with the medical arts and resist interpretation by medical science: spontaneous remission of advanced cancer, disappearance of trauma in tissue, awakening from months-long comas, regaining sight among the blind. And yes, contrary to the sneering dismissal of Hume, people do experience clinical death followed by resuscitation. One need not argue that all or any of these are due to direct divine intervention in order to recognize how much the world of human experience is filled with "signs and wonders" that confound the construal of reality as subject to inexorable laws and predictable outcomes.

Literalistic Reading

Along with a rationalistic approach to the world around them, Enlightenment thinkers cultivated a literalistic reading of texts (Frei 1980). Whether the stories they dealt with were from their neighbors or from Scripture, they preferred explanation to interpretation; that is, rather than ask first about the *meaning* of a statement or narrative, they asked about the *truth* of the account, with truth understood in terms of referentiality: does the story correspond to the extratextual facts (Preus 2009)? In ordinary discourse about the world, the truth of a statement, they were convinced, can be tested empirically. The claim "My house was struck by lightning,"

40

for example, is capable of being verified or nonverified. The claim "I have been healed by God through the laying on of hands," in contrast, cannot be verified; we may be able to prove that prior state of illness and the state of wellness afterward, but it is impossible to demonstrate the critical causal claim "by God."

Likewise, and to an even greater degree, the conviction expressed by Scripture that Jesus "went about doing good and healing all who were oppressed by the devil, for God was with him" (Acts 10:38), is in principle nonverifiable by appeal to empirical evidence. The final clause especially, "God was with him," escapes examination of anything within the empirical realm, for all agree at least on this, that "God" is not an object among other objects in the world.

A historical-critical reading of the Gospels, therefore, is necessarily reductive since history, as a way of knowing, can only deal with human events in past time and space that are at least potentially verifiable. The historical reading about miracles ascribed to Jesus and the apostles is consequently obliged to bracket the divine explanation in these stories since such causality is impossible to demonstrate, and such reading must focus instead on a range of explanations at the level of human causality. Thus miracle stories may be accounted for by human ignorance (of true causes) or superstition: they are explained in terms of human error. Alternatively, miracle stories are deliberately crafted in order to deceive others (fraud) or seduce followers (propaganda): they are explained in terms of human vice. Or they are composed out of religious convictions that seek to override the facts on the ground: they are explained in terms of human myth-making. Miracles are thus "explained" by being explained away: what "really happened" is something other than reported in the narrative.

The same approach is automatically applied to contemporary accounts of miracles as well. The number of cases in which sleight of hand and deception have played a role—and have been uncovered—in the history of religious phenomena, and the number of times such deception has been used to support the lowest of human drives—all this makes a "hermeneutics of suspicion" with regard to miracles the default enlightened position: the preponderance of evidence would seem to support fakery and fraud as the more probable explanation for such narratives, rather than a genuine experience of divine power.

41

The pertinent question is whether such literalistic reading of miracle accounts both in contemporary life and in Scripture is the best way of reading, or whether there might be a "hermeneutics of generosity" open to narratives about signs and wonders that are truthful with respect to the human experience of divine power and presence, apart from the issue of factual accuracy or verifiability, which may in fact not be the most important dimension of such accounts. In order to open that question, it will be necessary to think a bit more clearly about the ways in which stories might be both meaningful and true, by expanding the notion of truth beyond the narrow bounds of referentiality. This possibility, too, will be taken up in the next chapter.

Conclusion

The framing of the discussion of miracles by the Enlightenment of the eighteenth century, followed by centuries of increasing secularization, have created a crisis in Christian consciousness. This crisis touches not only on the accounts concerning miracles in Scripture or in the contemporary world, but also on the central elements of the Christian creed: if it is not possible to speak meaningfully about God's power and presence in creation through signs and wonders, neither is it possible to profess with integrity the incarnation of God's Son, or the resurrection and exaltation of Jesus as Lord, or the future judgment awaiting humanity. Some still calling themselves Christian embrace the Enlightenment framework fully and are content to squeeze some form of diminished Christianity within it. Many others, especially those trained in mainline seminaries, find themselves in a state of double-mindedness, wanting to profess the truths of the creed but unable in their pastoral practice simply and wholeheartedly to engage the mysteries of God's continuing presence in the world.

Unless present-day Christians can find their way back to a singleness of vision concerning God's presence and power in the world—until they can engage the empirical world as much in terms of mystery as of problem—they will continue to find the accounts of miracles in the Gospels a stumbling block, not only to the truths they state concerning Jesus but also to the truths they disclose concerning God's work in the present. In the final section of this chapter, I

42

have suggested some ways in which the default Enlightenment view of miracles is itself deeply problematic: its naïveté concerning "laws of nature," its overconcentration on individual acts, its inadequate conception of nature and its relation to humans, and its literalistic reading of narratives. But something far more than picking away at the secular position is required; Christians need a conversion of the imagination, a way of construing reality that does not depend on the dominant secular vision—even in order to criticize it—but instead replaces it altogether (Hays 2005). In the next chapter, I suggest an alternative approach to the perception of God's presence and power in the world: this approach is through imagining the world that Scripture imagines, specifically via a robust understanding of creation; through an appreciation of personal witness; and through a richer appreciation for the truth quality of biblical narratives.

CHAPTER 3

Reframing the Discussion

The secular construction of reality is powerful. It shapes both the discourse and practice of what we have come to call the First World. Within this construction, miracles find no place. Secularity is so pervasive and persuasive that it significantly influences even those who are explicitly committed to the Christian faith. The more that clergy and laity alike are educated within the frame of secularism, which dominates all higher education, the more likely they are to exhibit what the Letter of James calls "double-mindedness" (Jas. 1:8; 4:8): with one side of their brain they affirm the truths of faith; with another side of their brain they place large quotation marks around subjects like miracles, to indicate doubt or even derision.

Such double-mindedness, I have suggested, attaches itself as well to the fundamental convictions of the creed. Double-minded Christians profess faith in the incarnation but insist on measuring the incarnate Jesus of the Gospels through historical analysis; they profess belief in the continuing presence of the resurrected and exalted Lord but bracket that conviction in their perception of ordinary life. Incarnation and resurrection are as difficult to accept by the mind conditioned by a secular vision of the world as are the signs and wonders ascribed to the saints.

Restoring a vision of the world that enables both the testimony of Scripture and the witness of continuing human experience to be heard with full integrity is not easy. Pointing out the inadequacies

45

of the secular construction of the world is insufficient. If the statements of the creed and the witness of the saints are to be appreciated as something more than ancient errors or superstitious twaddle, an alternative and equally coherent vision is required. In this chapter I propose to sketch four elements of such an alternative vision, the recovery of which will allow a fresh approach to the miracle passages of Scripture and to the claims of miracles in the contemporary world. They are a rehabilitation of imagination as the essential organ of cognition, a renewed sense of creation as the continuous self-disclosure of God in the world, a recognition of the revelatory capacity of human somatic experience, and an appreciation of the particular way mythic narratives communicate truth.

Imagining the World That Scripture Imagines

The epistemological inadequacy of the secular construction of the world is linked to its restriction of authentic knowledge to a single set of mental processes applied to material objects and the interactions among them, and its banishing of alternative modes of knowing to the epistemological rubbish heap. Thus "reason" is defined in terms of the accurate description of the things apprehended by the senses, their analysis, measurement, calculation, prediction, and control. Modes of cognition activated by poetry, art, and music do not count as real knowledge. What stems from fantasy and the imagination belong to the realm of the "not real" and therefore the "not serious."

As I acknowledged earlier, such an epistemological concentration, connected to the technology that is its natural and inevitable expression, has demonstrated its effectiveness across a wide range of fields. No one can doubt the astonishing leaps in knowledge made since the eighteenth century in the natural sciences, and to some extent also in the social sciences. Developments in physics, chemistry, and biology have enabled an unparalleled knowledge and control of the world around and within humans. The ever-more rapid expansion of information and medical technology places humans at the edge of a genuine mutation into creatures whose limbs and organs and very brain circuits are electronically enabled and interconnected.

46

Yet the very success of this epistemology has also revealed its severe limitations. It is obvious, for example, that science (to use that cover term) is much more successful at knowing the general than at knowing the particular; thus arises its privileging of statistics and "laws." Science is little calibrated to individual instances and exceptions. Medical science, for example, is dazzling in its success at describing the patterns and causes of disease in general, yet medical practice finds itself frequently stymied by individual instances of disease. It is also far more impressive in its capacity to describe and combat illness than in its capacity to describe and enable health. It is far more advanced in the technology of "fixing the body" through limb and organ repair and replacement than it is in the "healing of the person" afflicted with autoimmune conditions or pervasive and nonspecific pain. It is better at observing and correcting existing conditions than it is at predicting or controlling the outcomes of those conditions.

The so-called social sciences, in turn, are likewise far better at describing things than at controlling or predicting things. Political science can minutely analyze past elections yet be hopeless at prognosticating a current election; economics is good at assessing current trends but fails miserably at detecting future trends; sociology provides precise graphs for current population clusters but does not have a clue about future population distribution. Most obviously, psychology is moderately successful at analyzing the causes for present behavior but is unable to predict future behavior with similar precision.

In short, the more the secularist epistemology turns from the nonhuman to the human, the less useful it appears to be. Huge tracts of human experience lie outside the scan of secular reason. Human dreams, desires, and fantasies escape scientific inquiry and are therefore regarded (by that measure) to be unimportant, even though it can be argued that more human behavior is guided by creative fantasy than by rational analysis (Person 1995). Understanding of human emotions has not advanced markedly beyond Aristotle and Plutarch, and insight into human virtue and vice falls short of that offered by those ancient moral thinkers. Self-help books (and videos) dealing with everything from diet and exercise to economic prosperity and inner tranquility proliferate and thereby testify at once to the range of human concerns and needs untouched by

47

secular reasoning, and also to the amateurish character of the "wisdom" directed to those concerns and needs.

The situation is illuminated by the critical distinction drawn by the existentialist philosopher and playwright Gabriel Marcel between the realm of the problematic and the mysterious (Marcel 1976, 2001). Problems lie outside the human person and are potentially soluble: financial budgets, broken household goods, highway engineering—all these are problems. Problems should be faced with precisely the ideals of enlightenment reasoning: detachment, objectivity, cool analysis. It is unhelpful to be emotionally involved with quadratic equations. In contrast, mysteries by their very nature involve human subjects, and the effort to detach the self from them results in distortion. Human relationships, for example, inevitably involve persons as subjects and participants. If such relationships are treated as problems to be solved, they are distorted. Another sort of thinking is required, an intersubjective mode of reflection, if relationships are to be adequately engaged (Johnson 2015).

As with relationships among humans, so with each human person's relationship to their own body, possessions, sexuality, power, and, above all, death. Embodied human existence resists easy understanding precisely because it is so difficult to grasp where the sphere of the problematic ends and the sphere of the mysterious begins. Take possessions as an example: planning a budget involves possessions and straightforwardly represents a problem to be solved; but what "being and having" means for my self-worth and willingness to share is far more complex and entangled, requiring a mode of engagement more responsive and supple than problem solving (Johnson 2011). By treating everything as a problem to be solved and refusing even to acknowledge the realm of the mysterious, secular epistemology both fails to see large tracts of human existence and distorts what it does see by insisting that this is all there is to see.

The greatest deficiency of the secular construction of reality, in fact, is its refusal to recognize that it is in fact an imaginative construct rather than a straightforward perception of "how things are." By no means is the epistemological reduction effected by the Enlightenment simply natural or obvious. It consists first of all in an overall construal of reality as a material and self-contained system of interrelated causes, knowable exclusively through the senses. There is no room within this construal for God or spirit,

48

except in the most marginal and meaningless fashion. The difficulty of "converting" people from another construal of the world to this one, through the instrumentality of higher education, and the difficulty even for converts to sustain an appropriate epistemological detachment in all circumstances—all this difficulty suggests that something other than an obvious or straightforward use of reason is here involved.

If we grant that secular reason does a decent job of giving an account of the things that fit within its construction of the world yet must necessarily dismiss or distort the things that do not fit within that construal, we are free to ask whether there might be other imaginative constructions of the world that can legitimately be adopted, and then ask what kind of thinking best gives an account of the things that fall within that alternative construal.

Give secularity its due: what it is capable of doing, it does well. But while we might ask a mechanic to fix our automobile, we would be fools to ask him to repair our marriage. Likewise, we would not ask the tone-deaf to interpret a symphony or the unsighted to distinguish colors. We should therefore not expect those with no sense of God to interpret the things that pertain to God's presence and power. We would be fools to seek, within secularism, an adequate account of the world as deriving from and ordered to God; for secularism, by definition, is both unable to do so and deeply disinterested in giving such an account. But by no means should we therefore conclude that such an account cannot be given, still less that it would lack intellectual integrity concerning the things of which it can and does speak.

"Imaginative worlds" are not the same as imaginary worlds, that is, alternative universes with only the loosest connection to the one inhabited by the one imagining and incapable of being brought into real, physical existence (Johnson 1998a). By imaginative worlds, rather, I mean those conceptions of reality brought into being first through the imagination but then fully capable of being brought into physical realization through specific physical practices that embody that conception. It is an activity of the mind that does not describe what is there, but first imagines what could be there and then works to put it there. Once an imaginative world is revealed through concrete and specific practices, it is perceived as "real," and once it has been practiced long enough, it can even be perceived by its participants as "natural" or even obvious. These points

49

are basic to the sociology of knowledge (Berger and Luckmann 1967; Berger 1966).

It is because we can imagine a world called "education," for example, that we willingly attend lectures and read difficult books and take exams (as students), or lecture and grade papers and exams (as teachers). By performing these practices, in turn, we make the world of education more real. Conversely, skipping classes and cheating on exams makes the plausibility structure of education less real; such social constructions depend on the wholehearted collusion of all participants to achieve a standing in the world. In like manner, it is because we can imagine a political system called democracy that we petition and vote or campaign and serve, and by such practices we make a government by the people, of the people, and for the people something more than a figment of imagination. People really do learn things in education and change the shape of things; people really do leave office when outvoted and thereby confirm the imaginative world of free citizens.

Indeed, science itself is best thought of in terms of such social construction. The greatest breakthroughs in science have been achieved, not by the techniques of bench workers, but by the fantasies of great dreamers. Copernicus and Einstein were great scientists not because they followed tried-and-true "methods" but because they imagined things in a way no one previously imagined. Before space travel was possible, humans needed to imagine the world in a new way, more like Copernicus and less like Ptolemy, more like Einstein and less like Newton. Once the possibility of standing on the moon was imagined, then the technologies of rocket engineering and space aeronautics made that possibility real in a fully embodied fashion.

With respect to the Bible, I am recommending what we generally recognize as axiomatic concerning the human project: we do not simply "find" a world, but together we construct worlds on the basis of shared imagination, and we engage in shared practices that serve to make what we imagine as both real and "natural." Certainly Scripture can be read as a set of compositions that in some sense describe the world. It can be read as a source of history, albeit with considerable difficulty. But the Copernican revolution I suggest means reading the Bible not for the accuracy of its description but for the power of its vision, seeking in its compositions not information about the world that produced Scripture, but the way in which

50

Scripture itself creates, through imagination, a world that might be inhabited. It means approaching Scripture not as an anthology of accidently gathered compositions locked in the past, but as a set of compositions that individually and as a collection speaks a word that unlocks every present; not as an inadequate collection of historical sources that poorly describe reality, but as a set of witnesses that powerfully prescribe reality; not as an assortment of propositions about the world, but as an imaginative construction of a world within which humans can choose to live, a world they can embody through practices consistent with that vision.

It is too seldom observed that in each and every one of its parts, and as a whole, Scripture imagines a world as created by and ordered to, cared for and saved by, a God who is at once infinitely powerful and infinitely personal; a world in which this God creates humans in God's own image, with capacities for knowledge and love, pleasure and freedom; a world that is imaged as a garden that God plants for humans to enjoy and cultivate. Nothing about this imagined world is empirically verifiable. Yet by imagining the empirical world we all inhabit in this fashion, the Bible also reveals a world, and by revealing it, opens as well the possibility of humans living in it as though real. By imagining the world that Scripture imagines, humans can receive and engage their own world as God's new creation.

Our reluctance to adopt this "Copernican" shift in perspective—abandoning an obsession with historical evidence in favor of a utopian vision—has something to do with the hegemony, even among believers, of secularity's epistemological reduction. When truth is attached only to propositions that are empirically verifiable, through natural science or critical history, then imagination appears as epistemologically unserious, perhaps even irresponsible. Yet, as I have suggested, all great historiography and all great science are certainly grounded in fantasy and imagination before being expressed through test tubes and textual criticism, just as every interesting human life is driven by fantasy and imagination far more than by the analysis of facts.

But there is also a moral factor in the reluctance, even among believers, to embrace this way of engaging Scripture, for it demands of readers a willingness to put into practice the world thus imagined by the Bible. If the Bible is "true" as description (or prediction), it demands nothing of readers beyond intellectual assent; its truth is

51

like that of a weather report or algebraic equation. But if the Bible is true as prescription, then everything is demanded of readers: they are called on to see reality in a new way, to embody that vision, to bring it into physical existence through practices consonant with it. Even Christians are understandably reluctant to commit themselves so wholeheartedly to that which is simply "imaginative."

Just as the secularist construal of reality has both an overall perception of what is real (things can be apprehended by the senses) and specific applications (quantitative measurement), so does the world shaped by scriptural imagination have an overall perception of what is real, together with specific applications. Rather than reality being confined to material things interconnected in a closed system of cause and effect, the biblical imagination conceives of reality as including things unseen as well as seen, an open system whose source and goal is an unseen power active in things both seen and unseen. In this sense, the biblical world is larger and more comprehensive than that imagined by a Hume or even a Stephen Hawking, for it includes not only spiritual dimensions, but also the living God (Johnson 1998a).

Secularists (and demythologizers) find it easy to mock the "three-decker" cosmology imagined by Scripture. But readers both ancient and modern have used such biblical language to understand not the vertical physical structure of the universe, but rather the richness and depth of the visible world. Is there only the surface that we can see and touch and measure, or is that surface a veil, behind which is a deeper and more authentic form of being? It is astonishing (but logical) that even some contemporary students of religion subscribe to modernity's epistemological reduction: "For me, things are surface; there simply is no depth; there is simply no original; and there is no concealment. It's all out there, it's plain, it's ordinary, it's largely uninteresting, and it's utterly—in fact overwhelmingly, that's the problem for the scholar—accessible" (J. Smith 1987, 211).

But in truth, the language of heaven and earth enables readers to "see" a world that does not offer itself easily to immediate comprehension, but rather discloses itself slowly to those who are open to the mystery that lies beneath the surface. We can, in fact, reverse the proposition: without a language that enables us to imagine inner and outer dimensions of human existence, or a sense of height and depth in being, is not our apprehension of the world, and

52

particularly of humanity, inevitably flattened and rendered banal (Chesterton 1908 = 1959, 14–29)? This overall perception also has specific applications. Scripture, for example, imagines humans as created in the image of God. This is a way of "seeing" humanity that is certainly not derived from the observation of human behavior, and is certainly not empirically verifiable. Yet if humans actually imagine each other as bearing a divine impress, and if they act on that perception, they can discover that a truth empirically unverifiable can be empirically embodied.

God as Creator

That God creates the world is the most fundamental of the convictions of faith. First of all it is fundamental for the rest of the Christian narrative to make sense. Because God is the source of all things, God can also be revealer, savior, sanctifier, and judge of all things. Because heaven and earth are not God, but come from God's power at every moment, by their very existence they reveal the one who makes them (Wis. 13:1–9; Rom. 1:19–20). Because God has "maker's knowledge" of all that exists—that is, knows all things from within—God can judge righteously as One who discerns the heart (Acts 1:24) and cannot be swayed by appearances (1 Pet. 1:17). Because God loves what he has made, God seeks to save his world (Pss. 65:1–13; 79:9; 1 Tim. 2:4). Because the universe is the bodily expression of God's Spirit, God by his Holy Spirit is able to transform the world and sanctify it (Ps. 51:1–17; Rom. 15:16; 2 Thess. 2:13).

The conviction is fundamental as well because it most decisively divides humans in their most basic disposition toward the world in which they find themselves. The real divide is between atheists and believers. Deists and agnostics fall on either side of the divide because they neither affirm nor deny anything very important. A Deist's God who once wound up the world like a clock and then let it tick on its own may be praised or blamed for good or poor craftsmanship but in no manner resembles the God professed as maker of heaven and earth by Jews, Christians, and Muslims. As for agnostics, their posture of intellectual rigor and detachment masks moral confusion: humans cannot remain detached concerning the most pressing of existential questions, as though

53

God were a hypothesis still requiring more data to be satisfactorily demonstrated, and we were only mildly interested observers in the outcome.

Atheists, in turn, seldom adopt their position because they have acquired a superior level of scientific knowledge, although science sometimes serves as a legitimation for a stance that derives from moral rather than a purely intellectual stance. There is a long tradition of "noble atheists" who refuse to acknowledge the existence of an all-powerful and loving God precisely because of the perceived savagery in nature ("red in tooth and claw," says Alfred Lord Tennyson, *In Memoriam*, canto 56, https://allpoetry.com/In -Memoriam-A.-H.-H.:-56) and the depressing evidence of cruelty and evil among humans. As memorably stated by Voltaire, "God's only excuse is that he does not exist." Such atheists regard belief in a creator God as a craven relinquishment of human freedom and moral responsibility (Lubac 1944 = 1995).

Other atheists, to be sure, are less noble. They are named by the Bible as the fools who say in their heart, "There is no God" (Pss. 10:4; 14:1), precisely as an excuse to exercise their freedom in moral irresponsibility. Hence Dostoyevsky had one of his characters state, "If there is no God, then all things are permitted" (*The Brothers Karamasov* 4.11.4). Neither is such atheism the result of scientific reasoning: it derives rather from the willful denial of human contingency and the assertion of a false independence.

On the other side of the divide are those who profess belief in a creator God. Such belief is also not based in any sort of scientific inquiry, but it finds expression in three kinds of language: that of the Christian creed, that of Scripture, and that of the human heart.

The Nicene Creed, the most widely used expression of Christian faith, provides a starting point: "We believe in one God, the Father Almighty, maker of heaven and earth, of all things, visible and invisible." Even the minority of Christians who find creeds generally unpalatable will subscribe to this statement as representing their own belief. I hope that they would also agree to two further observations concerning this declaration. The first is that the creed is a communal and public profession, rather than an individual and private one. The person who recites the creed with others during worship thereby declares an allegiance not only to the truth of the proposition, but also to all the other people who affirm that same proposition, acknowledging as well that at any given moment the

54

church as a whole believes more and better than any individual member of the church. The second is that the language of the creed is performative: those who recite it *profess* the conviction that God is the source and goal of their own existence and their commitment to live in a manner consonant with their profession (Johnson 2003).

The creed, in turn, derives from and provides a guide to reading the much more complex language of Scripture. All Christians would agree that the specific language shaping their view of creation, which the creed reduces to a proposition, is the rich and variegated language of the Old and New Testaments concerning God as the source and goal of all that exists. The language of Scripture is indeed rich, but it is also irreducibly diverse.

Scripture is diverse first of all because its compositions were written by humans across many centuries and lands, thus reflecting the linguistic and cultural particularities of the times and places of composition. Christians affirm the divine inspiration of Scripture, to be sure, but that affirmation is connected to the equally important one that, as the creed says, the Holy Spirit "spoke through the prophets": the human Moses, Isaiah, David, Solomon, and Paul gave specific and finite expression to the Word that God wanted humans to hear and obey. Because of its historical and cultural rootedness, therefore, Scripture contains distinct witnesses concerning everything from creation to incarnation to eschatology, witnesses whose value is found precisely in the fact that they do not agree at every point. We are not astonished, then, to find one sort of witness to God's creative activity in the first chapter of Genesis, another in the second chapter, and still others in the Psalms and Prophets.

The language of Scripture is diverse also because its compositions speak in a variety of modes. Some are narratives of a quasi-historical character, while others are clearly legendary or mythic. Some parts of Scripture consist of law. Other parts speak in the form of prayer, poetry, prophecy, or proverb, and in these modes the metaphorical is always dominant. It is an abuse of Scripture to reduce all these modes to one, and above all to literalize and thereby kill Scripture's metaphors. Despite all this diversity, it is also true that on the points that matter most, that pertain to imagining the world, Scripture's many witnesses speak with a remarkable consistency. Indeed, this is one of the small miracles that make us think of the Bible as inspired: written by so many different people over so

55

many centuries and social settings, Scripture nevertheless imagines a world that is internally consistent and satisfyingly coherent.

As stated in the preceding paragraphs, I use the term "imagines" advisedly. Scripture does not so much describe the empirical world that is the realm of scientific hypothesis and demonstration as it imagines a world that at every moment derives from and is directed to one ultimate power. Because it so imagines the world, Scripture also reveals this world as permeable to and penetrated by that divine power. By so revealing the world, Scripture also invites its readers to share that imaginative vision and to render it empirically through practices consistent with its vision of reality. Because goodness, beauty, and truth exist in some degree among humans, Scripture imagines their maker as perfect in the possession of goodness, beauty, and truth, and so imagines humans—all empirical evidence to the contrary notwithstanding—as created in the image of their maker. But wonder of wonders, even though wickedness, ugliness, and deception also exist among humans, Scripture does not ascribe these qualities to the Creator; instead, all that God makes is good, "very good" (Gen. 1:31), and God is imagined as faithful and compassionate and righteous in every respect.

The third language that comes into play in Christian faith in God as creator is the language of the heart. I do not mean simply feeling or sentiment. When the Bible speaks of the human heart, it refers to the seat of thought and discernment, of decision and of moral disposition (see Gen. 6:5; 8:21; 27:41 [KJV]; Exod. 4:21; Deut. 2:30; 4:39; Pss. 14:1; 16:9; 17:3; 22:26; Jer. 17:9–10). Blaise Pascal drew on this dimension when he declared, "The heart has its reasons, which reason does not know" (*Pensées*, no. 277, http://www.leaderu.com/cyber/books/pensees/pensees-SECTION-4.html). The heart in this sense points to the deepest and most obscure mystery of human freedom: just as the noble atheist looks at the world and finds it lacking either logic or mercy, so does the believer gaze on the world and find it drenched with grace. Who knows how, or why?

We cannot account for the tangle of causes that lead to such different perceptions. We do not know why one person can place a finger to her pulse and feel the power of God, while another can feel only the movement of blood. What we can say is that it is the language of the heart within the believer that makes the language of the Bible sensible, even compelling, and makes the language of the creed something gladly to embrace, while the atheist finds the language of the Bible unintelligible when not obscure, and regards the creed a perfect example of intellectual vacuity. The believer finds congruence among the three languages. The atheist finds a dire dissonance between the first two and what the heart declares.

Christian thinking about God as creator—an activity distinct from believing in and obeying God as creator—starts with and never moves far from the language of Scripture, but such thinking often suffers from two interrelated errors. The first is to take the opening chapters of Genesis as though they were the only pertinent texts; the second is to reduce the stunningly imaginative vision of Genesis to a literalism that simultaneously robs it of poetry and diminishes the force of its witness. The best way to avoid the second error is by eliminating the first.

Each of the two creation accounts in Genesis has its own beauty and power. Genesis 1 tells us that God is not to be identified with the world or with part of the world, but rather is the originator of all that exists in the world; that God brings everything into being by a commanding word; that creation is therefore ordered and declared good as God makes it. Humans are created in the image and likeness of God, male and female participating equally in that image and likeness, and equally exercising dominion over other creatures. Genesis 1 declares human sexuality good by making the propagation of children the first divine commandment to humans. This vision of creation is majestic, the unfolding of a cosmic drama, with God orchestrating each stage of the process—and it is a process—through his command, his internal counsel ("Let us make man"), and his approving comment ("It is good").

The creation account in Genesis 2 has its own distinctive perspective, equally imaginative and powerful. Here God is much more intimately involved with his creation, forming a human from the dust of the earth, placing him in a garden to tend and preserve it, parading the animals before Adam to receive names and possibly to find a mate for the man, expressing empathy ("It is not good for man to be alone"), shaping a partner for him from the male's rib. In this version, the narrator focuses on the relationship between male and female (they cleave to each other) more than their propagation of children, and on the imposition of limits to what they may eat in the garden, introducing the possibility of obedience or disobedience in creation.

57

Taken together, the Genesis creation accounts express a wisdom that speaks inexhaustibly to the human condition, not only as it was "in the beginning," but above all as it continues to be in every circumstance throughout time. It is not at all strange that these accounts are echoed in the paeans to personified wisdom in Proverbs 8 and Sirach 24—and in the prologue to John's Gospel!—for they have occupied sages in the Jewish and Christian tradition for centuries, constantly enriching those who invest their minds, and especially their imaginations, in the study of these passages. The list extends from Philo of Alexandria (*Allegorical Interpretation*) to Leon Kass (2004), and beyond.

When these marvelous accounts are isolated from other voices within Scripture and read in an inappropriately literalistic fashion, however, they are deprived of their power precisely to the degree that they are robbed of their magic. The perils of reading the start of Genesis as though it were a historical or scientific description are illustrated by Augustine of Hippo, who tried three times to interpret Genesis "according to the letter"—in contrast to his usual allegorical approach—and failed to make any real progress. Augustine kept getting stuck (Johnson and Kurz 2002, 102–8).

From our vantage point, we can see that Augustine's frustration was due to his lack of appreciation for narrative truth that would enable him to engage the metaphorical qualities of the accounts on their own terms. As soon as one tries to parse the first chapter along the lines of the temporality of "days," the spatial arrangement of "firmaments," and the distinctions of plants and animals, as though these were matters of natural science, one loses the point of the account altogether. And the second chapter is worse: how can one speak literally of humans made from dust or a rib? Such conceptions do not defy theories of evolution: they do not even rise to the level of basic human biology. Only people who are simultaneously desperate to maintain the truth of the Bible and reduce the truth of narrative to the purely referential can commit such grievous offenses against intellectual integrity as to seek science in these poetic tales.

The temptation to literalize the poetry of Genesis 1–2 increases as these chapters are isolated from other scriptural witnesses and treated as though they alone speak to the subject of God's creating activity. In fact, these chapters are neither the only nor the most important scriptural witnesses. But when they receive exclusive attention, creation appears as an event that happened in the distant past (rather than also in the present); the text is read as a chronological beginning rather than as an existential cause, and therefore is read as something that has concluded rather than continuing. In short, when isolated and read literally, Genesis 1–2 can be used to support precisely the Deist conception of a god who is around to get things started and then leaves creation to its own devices. In this conception, as we have seen, "miracles" must therefore be an exception to those "natural laws" that were established in the beginning, rather than evidence for the continuing and constant presence and power of the Creator.

Other voices in Scripture, in contrast, suggest that God's creative activity never ceases. Psalm 104, for example, celebrates creation as a wonder that God performs new every day. God summons and controls the forces of nature, establishes and maintains the boundaries of the universe, calls into being and nourishes plants and animals. God does all this, not once for all, but continuously:

> These all look to you to give them their food in due season; when you give to them, they gather it up; when you open your hand, they are filled with good things. When you hide your face, they are dismayed; when you take away their breath, they die and return to their dust. When you send forth your spirit, they are created; and you renew the face of the ground. May the glory of the LORD endure forever; may the LORD rejoice in his works— who looks on the earth and it trembles, who touches the mountains and they smoke. . . . Bless the LORD, O my soul. Praise the LORD! (Ps. 104:27–35)

This God creates the world new at every moment and is totally present to the changing world because it is by his power that it comes into being and changes.

In the prophetic literature we find a similar congruence between God's continuing creative power and his shaping events in history. Thus Isaiah mingles the language of creation and of new creation in history. The Lord who makes the world and humans (45:8–12) also "makes the things to come" (44:7) and makes things new (Isa. 43:19; 48:6). Isaiah links God's creative energies in the beginning, his constant renewal of the earth, and his work within human events:

59

> Thus says God, the LORD, who created the heavens and stretched them out, who spread out the earth and what comes from it, who gives breath to the people upon it and spirit to those who walk in

it: I am the LORD, I have called you in righteousness, I have taken
you by the hand and kept you; I have given you as a covenant to
the people, a light to the nations. . . . I am the LORD, that is my
name. (Isa. 42:5–8)

In the New Testament, God's continuing creative activity is
connected above all to the resurrection of Jesus from the dead; Paul
declares of Abraham, "He is the father of all of us, . . . in the presence of the God in whom he believed, who gives life to the dead
and calls into existence the things that do not exist" (Rom. 4:16–17).
For Paul, Jesus' resurrection amounts to a "new creation" (2 Cor.
5:17; Gal. 6:15). Christ is the "last Adam" (1 Cor. 15:45), who is the
"new human" (Col. 3:10 AT), by whose image other humans are
measured and into whose image the Holy Spirit shapes believers
(2 Cor. 5:17–18). Paul blends creation and resurrection language
when he declares, "The God who said, 'Let light shine out of dark-
ness,' . . . has shone in our hearts to bring to light the knowledge of
the glory of God in the face of Jesus Christ" (2 Cor. 4:6 AT).

The resurrection of Jesus and the renewal of humanity (Rom.
12:1–2) is not the end of God's creative activity. The book of Revelation joins the first creation to the new creation. In Revelation
14:7, we read, "Worship him who made heaven and earth, the sea
and the springs of water," and in 21:1–5, we find the vision of the
full realization of the new creation: "Then I saw a new heaven and a
new earth; for the first heaven and the first earth had passed away,
and the sea was no more. . . . And the one who was seated on the
throne said, 'See, I am making all things new.'"

Likewise 2 Peter 3:13, in turn, declares, "In accordance with
his promise, we wait for new heavens and a new earth, where righteousness is at home." In sum, the dominant testimony of Scripture
is that creation is not simply an event of the past, but a constant and
present activity of God.

In another place, I have used the expression "critical theological concepts" (Johnson 1990a, 15–30). By this I mean that while
we may not be able to provide an adequate account of the positive
content of a conviction of faith, we know that its denial distorts
essential truths by which we live. Here is an analogy: I may not be
able to demonstrate the ways or the degree to which my wife loves
me, but to deny that she loves me means distorting every aspect
of our life together. So now I turn to a series of short affirmations

60

spelling out the critical theological concept of creation that is stated propositionally by the creed, witnessed to poetically by Scripture, and testified to by the hearts of believers.

First, profession of God as creator is, as I have suggested, the supreme example of a critical theological concept. It is impossible for us to demonstrate the positive content of the proposition: through scientific analysis we cannot show that God creates the world, much less how it happens. But we stake our lives on this conviction, being convinced that denial of God's creating activity means distorting both the world and our place within it. We agree with Paul that the first and greatest lie is to refuse to acknowledge God's claim on us in our creaturely status, which leads to the systemic lies and distortions that corrupt human existence and lead creation itself into bondage (Rom. 1:18–32; 8:20).

Second, the phrase "in the beginning" (Gen. 1:1) must be thought of not in terms of time but in terms of causality. If "in the beginning" is understood solely in terms of chronology, then creation can also be considered as initiated and completed sometime in the distant past. In contrast, Scripture's witness focuses especially on God's Spirit moving through and stirring the world as the "life-giver" who brings all things into existence at every moment. God is the world's "beginning" not just once long ago but especially at every moment.

Third, Scripture and the human heart also attest to the truth that God's creative activity continues as the fundamental sustaining and shaping power at work in all things, as the cause that causes all other causes. God as life-giver always moves ahead of the processes of the empirical world because at every moment of every empirical process, God's power is at work. God as creator is not, as some have supposed, like the first in a series of secondary causes, which demands, as Bertrand Russell complained, an infinite regress (1927). Rather, God's creative activity is the cause simultaneously (so to speak) underlying the entire series of secondary causes.

Fourth, the Christian confession of God as creator is therefore not a theory about *how* things came and come into existence, but rather a perception *that* all things are always and at every moment coming into existence. God's self-disclosure in and through creation, therefore, is not adequately compared to the traces of the watchmaker in a watch. God is revealed most of all not in the *what-ness* of things, their essence, but in the *isness* of things, their very

61

existence. That anything exists at all, that there should be anything rather than not be anything, is the primordial mystery that points us to God.

Fifth, everything that exists, insofar as it exists, is capable of revealing God. Although they differ in size and significance, a mouse and a mountain reveal the implicit presence of the creating God in the same way, by their explicit coming-into-being in the world. The smallest cell and the largest stellar constellation are equally fragile, equally dependent on God for their existence. Likewise every human breath, impulse, and movement is dependent on God's creative presence, and that state of contingency, of real but nonnecessary existence derived from another, never changes into a more secure condition, not for mountains, not for humans. All that is constantly comes into and moves out of existence, while the one who breathes through them all alone remains necessary and sufficient.

Sixth, all that is sensible in the world—every material thing that presses upon us and that we engage in our daily rounds—points beyond itself to an unseen power that brings it into existence. In this way the world itself, in all its creatures and all its processes, can be regarded as God's chosen instrument of self-revelation. Spirit needs body for its expression, and the world itself in its contingent existence, in its continual coming-into-existence, can be regarded as the body God has chosen to express his own spirit (Johnson 2015, 36–85). God's revelation is not something that takes place outside the world's processes but precisely and necessarily through them, through the shape of leaf and branch, through the swim of blood in the veins, through the dance of eroticism, through the gestures and words of the prophets.

Seventh, humans are called to see God's creative activity at work in every worldly process and event, in the coming-into-being of all that comes to be. This means that humans are called to see the miraculous everywhere and in everything. Everything that exists is wondrous and ultimately inexplicable in worldly terms, precisely in its existence. The miraculous is not, as modernity would have it, an exception to the well-established laws of nature, but is rather the magic of God's power and presence, whose laws or logic humans must struggle to decipher. Within this framework, a healing worked by medical art is just as much a miracle as healing accomplished through prayer, for existence in all its forms is equally a surprising and gracious demonstration of the power of God. Christians shaped by this scriptural imagination correctly perceive the effort by secularism to demystify the world as erroneous, as an idolatrous effort to adopt a set of mechanical explanations to replace the beauty and mystery inherent in the veiled dance called existence.

Eighth, this vision of creation—a vision supported by the entire weight of scriptural witness—is entirely compatible with theories of evolution, for it sees God's world as always in the process of becoming, never finished once-for-all, always flowing from the infinite creative energies of an all-powerful giver of life. Theories of astronomy and geology and biology that enable us to perceive a universe immeasurably more vast than earlier ages had imagined, an earth far more constantly in ferment from the eruption of volcanos and the clash of tectonic plates than we had appreciated until very recently, and an ecology far more complexly developed and more fragilely interconnected than people before us had realized: all these scientific perspectives address and can only address the interlocking causes and effects of beings that have been or are now already in existence. They cannot account for existence itself, for the fact that anything at all should be rather than not be, for the reality that all things together hang dependently on a power not their own (individually or collectively). Concerning the sequence of becoming, however, scientific theories touching on an expanding universe and evolving species are actually more congruent with the scriptural witness concerning the ever-creating God than is the antiquated science of static and stable entities set forever in an unchanging order.

Ninth, the understanding of creation sketched here does not in the least preclude responsible discourse concerning the "signs and wonders" through which God's power and presence in creation are made more explicit. In fact, the implicit power and presence of the Creator in all the world's processes is the necessary premise for those events and experiences that come to be designated by humans as "miracles." Claims to the experience of such signs and wonders are not based on the supposition that God is otherwise absent from the world; rather, they propose that God's implicit presence and power has, in this instance, been experienced in a more direct and explicit fashion. Thus as the Prologue to John's Gospel claims, the incarnation of God's word in Jesus, as well as the acts he performed for his fellow humans, as well as his resurrection from the dead, all reveal "the light . . . that was in the world" through him as God's "glory," which could be perceived by those gazing with the eyes of faith (John 1:1–14). In the world Jesus indeed "expressed" the God whom no human eye can see and made his "glory," that is, God's presence and power, palpable (John 1:18). The same is the case with the signs and wonders worked through the intervention of the saints, and through the skill of human doctors: the truth that lies always implicitly behind the veil of appearances is for a moment disclosed and made explicit. But to better comprehend how this happens, we need to consider two further things: revelation as a process of human interpretation and the character of religious narrative.

Revelation as a Process of Interpretation

Secularism validates knowledge that is public and proven, verifiable through empirical testing. The goal is the establishment of universal laws that are, given the proper methods and the appropriate dispositions of detached rationality, accessible to all who are not shackled by superstition. Claims to truth that are based only on personal experience are suspect precisely because they are subjective, idiosyncratic, and, therefore, unreliable. Even on its own terms, however, as I have tried to suggest, this secular construal has severe limits. It is clear first of all that the so-called laws of nature are not so much universally discerned and tested through the rational inquiry of individuals, as they are dogmas accepted by the many from the exceptional few whose genius or luck enabled them—on the basis of experience, after all—to construct such postulates. Moreover, as I have already suggested, such universal laws are of little use for the most important aspects of life: the big-bang theory of cosmic origins does not help with my family dynamics; evolutionary psychology may instruct me concerning trends in human mating but does not account for the mysterious attraction between my wife and myself; medical science can determine a disease that is mortal but offers no guidance for how I should face my death in a human manner.

64   Another perspective is both possible and necessary if we are to engage the dimensions of the mysterious that impinge on every human existence but that are occluded by the strictures of

Enlightenment epistemology. This perspective is based on the conviction that humans have experiences opening them to a depth of reality not given by surface appearances, that such experiences represent genuine (and necessarily) subjective knowledge, and that witness borne to such experience and knowledge deserves as much a hearing as do the claims made by those who base themselves solely on empirical phenomena. This perspective is that of divine revelation.

I argue here that God discloses his power implicitly in the processes of the world, which is the arena of our common human experience; that such self-disclosure is never obvious and self-validating and is always capable of being denied; that some human experiences manifest God's presence and power in more explicit ways, but never unambiguously; that every such experience is inevitably clothed in the symbols available to the one experiencing; and that such experience involves a process of interpretation not only afterward but also during the experience itself (Johnson 1990a).

If we (properly) think of God in terms of spirit rather than in terms of an object among other objects, then it is clearly nonsense to propose that God could ever be perceived by humans "as God is," because our perceptions are always conditioned by the categories of time and space, which are not the qualities of "spirit." The scholastic axiom "Whatever is received is received according to the mode of the receiver" emphatically applies here (*quidquid recipitur modo recipientis recipitur*; Aquinas, *Summa theologiae* 1.75.5). Commonsense instances of the principle will find ready agreement: a blind eye does not receive light, a dry battery cannot be charged, a bucket cannot contain a lake. But likewise, someone with perfect musical pitch can both appreciate and be pained by musical performance to a degree unimaginable for those who are tone-deaf; someone who is color-blind can only guess at the nuances of tone perceived by those without this deficiency.

The same principle applies to the experience of God's presence and power; it also is inevitably fitted to the capacity of the one experiencing that presence and power. It follows that in this realm as well, some people have a greater capacity for certain kinds of experience than do others. It follows as well that those not similarly capable find it easy to distrust or deny such claims to experience. If my myopia causes me to be skeptical of the sharpshooter's claim to see for miles, and if my casual sense of pitch makes me doubt that

65

sharpness causes pain to one with absolute pitch, my captivity to a secular flattening of the world will also encourage me to suspect claims to perceive realities behind the surface phenomena available to all. Claims to experience the presence and power of God make sense only to those willing to trust the validity of subjective testimony and willing to recognize different degrees of openness to the mystery of existence.

Experience, however, is not only determined by psychological or spiritual capacity. It is equally shaped by the symbols available to us and how those symbols shape our perception. Three of us in the room may agree that we heard a loud noise, saw a flash of light, and felt surprised and startled; we agree that we all encountered something, which was real. But what was it? I state that it was thunder and lightning; you are convinced it was an angel; our mutual friend swears it is an unidentified flying object. The nature and significance even of a "shared" experience are constituted by the interpretation made possible by our respective symbolic worlds. Every human experience, however powerful, frightening, or transforming, is conditioned by human consciousness: we see and hear what our symbols enable us to see and hear.

There are, to be sure, cases in which experience is so new and so massive as to challenge our customary interpretations and shatter our operative symbolic world. The Holocaust was such an experience for some six million Jews exterminated by Nazi Germany simply because they were Jews. This was not garden-variety anti-Semitism, nor was it war in different terms. It was a *novum*—an utterly new combination of racial ideology and lethal technology that defied all previously known categories (Fackenheim 1991). The Holocaust was so awesome an experience—in reality countless "experiences" gathered under a single title—that for a period of time it silenced both participants and perpetrators and fragmented the symbolic world of traditional Judaism. But even so shocking an intrusion into "life as normal" is now, despite physical evidence and the eyewitness testimony of survivors, vigorously denied by some (Lipstadt 1994). By others, it is relativized, reevaluated, and reinterpreted, as other events succeed it and make it appear more as just another (though no less terrifying) event within history (Johnson 2002a).

66

Thus the term "revelation" more properly describes a process of human interpretation than a divine activity. In one sense, this conclusion places us in a position of relativism. It is impossible to validate any interpretation to everyone, or even prove the reality of an experience to those unable or unwilling to share the framework providing the interpretation. But the relativism is not total. In the first place, symbols are more or less adequate to receive certain experiences; a consciousness conditioned by symbols of transcendence is capable of experiencing the world in a manner impossible to a consciousness lacking such symbols. The symbol "angel," for example, enables perceptions that the symbol "thunder" does not.

In the second place, a given society may structure a group consciousness—both through its organization of the world and its explanations for the world—that either enables or forecloses certain kinds of experiences. A given social construction of reality can effectively preclude certain kinds of experiences: a symbolic world made up exclusively of interconnected material processes in a closed system of "natural laws" makes it difficult to experience the world as open, giving, surprising, revealing mysteries.

Such is the social construction within which the populations of the developed, industrialized, mechanized, and digitalized nations dwell. It is the secular world shaped by Enlightenment and Technology, a world that not only denies the possibility of God's existence and claim upon creation, but also works to structure a social consciousness within which such denial appears ever more plausible and "natural." In this world, speaking of transcendence appears odd, even crazy, for the success and stability of the given social consciousness is structured on (and has a stake in) the effective denial of transcendence. In this world, claims for the experience of miracles, claims for God's effective power and presence in creation, appear as alien and even threatening to the social order.

Just such an alternative symbolic world is offered by the Christian tradition, which speaks of a God who creates anew at every moment and who presses upon us in our encounters with empirical reality. It is a worldview that opens our consciousness, however indirectly, to the experience and perception of the divine presence and power in the world. It *enables* revelation by providing the symbols necessary for revelation. By providing such an alternative vision of the world, the creed and Scripture give humans the freedom—perilous though it is—to choose another way of inhabiting and engaging and interpreting empirical reality.

67

What validates the construal of experience as open to God and engaging God? Only the experience of the world that such construal enables, only the project of human freedom it engenders, only the sort of self and community it yields, only the finished person called the saint, only the ordering of human existence called the rule of God.

Because the secular vision of reality is so dominant and so aggressively reinforced by all social mechanisms, the cultivation of this alternative construal is essentially countercultural, requiring a community that asserts and practices, with at least equal vigor, the imaginative world of Scripture concerning God's constant creative activity and the possibility of God's presence and power being experienced through "signs and wonders," even of the most everyday sort. The strength of the scriptural vision is dependent on a robust community that shares its perception and lives according to its practices. The weakness of this vision in the contemporary world is directly connected to the church's failure to translate it into consistent practice.

The Truthfulness of Myth

Secularists are true heirs of the Enlightenment in their dismissal of myth as a species of falsehood associated with ignorance (of natural laws) and superstition. But the derogation of myth actually begins within the New Testament, which opposes the truth of the gospel to the "endless myths" of both Judaism and Gentile religion (see 1 Tim. 1:4; 4:7; Titus 1:14; 2 Pet. 2:16). What the authors of the New Testament were not in a position to recognize is the degree to which its own claims concerning God's power and presence were themselves mythic in character. In any case, the dismissal of myth as a species of falsehood goes hand in hand with the rejection of the miraculous. It was in order to secure a miracle-free version of the good news that "demythologization" of the New Testament itself was regarded as essential to secure a credible faith for "modern man," who supposedly dwells in a myth-free environment (Kraftchick 2014). It follows, then, that an enthusiastic embrace of God's presence and power in creation through "signs and wonders" demands a positive appreciation of myth as the distinctive mode of speaking truth concerning realities for which science and philosophy have no adequate language.

Since the nature and function of myth is hotly debated, it is best to begin with a working definition. By "myth" I mean first-order statements, often but not necessarily in the form of a narrative, that place human and divine persons in situations of mutual agency (Johnson 2014). Since human agency is involved, such statements claim to be about the same empirical world that we all perceive; but because divine agency is also and even primarily involved, such statements also resist ordinary empirical verification. Certain points need to be made about such statements: They are absolutely necessary not only for believers to talk about miracles but even for them to express any of the truths by which they live. Myth is not nonsensical or arbitrary but reveals a genuine logic and connectedness to the human experience of the world. And myths can be tested, even if not by the instruments of natural science.

The first point is illustrated in Paul's Letters. In 2 Corinthians, for example, Paul's extraordinarily dense language intertwines the specific empirical circumstances of himself and his readers with the work of God in Christ (I am using my own translation in this analysis). In 5:19, he declares that "God was in Christ reconciling the world to himself." The Greek can be read either ontologically ("God was in Christ") or instrumentally ("through Christ God was reconciling"). But in either case the mythic quality of this narrative fragment is the same. Although Paul is undoubtedly referring to the historical figure Jesus of Nazareth, nothing in this statement is empirically verifiable: "Christ," "God," "world," and "reconciling" are not locatable among the material objects of everyday life. The statement is most clearly mythic because it ascribes causality directly to God within the frame of worldly existence. In 5:18, Paul provides a parallel version: "All things are from God, who was reconciling *us* to himself through Christ."

When we look more closely at the immediate context of Paul's declaration in 2 Corinthians 5:1–21, we see how complexly he weaves together several registers of language. Some fourteen statements have humans as their subject and refer entirely to human actions and dispositions: we "are groaning" (5:2), "longing" (5:2), "burdened and groaning" (5:4), "are sober" (5:13), "beg" (5:20), and so forth. There is another statement in the first-person singular ("I hope that," 5:11) and one in the third-person plural ("those who boast in appearance," 5:12). In all these, agency clearly belongs to Paul, his associates, and his rivals, even if it is carried out "before God" (5:13); we are in the realm of the ordinary affairs of the world.

69

Five other statements in the same passage have quite a different character: the "we" is here the recipient of action or disposition, and God or Christ is the agent. The empirical "we" is placed in realms beyond the empirical. Thus we "have a building from God, a dwelling not made with hands, eternal in heaven" (5:1), "have been given the Spirit as a first installment" (5:5), "must all appear before the judgment seat of Christ" (5:10), are "in Christ a new creation" (5:17), are "reconciled to God" (5:18). Unlike the first set, none of the referents here can be found in the arena of ordinary human discourse. They suppose an understanding of reality that includes what cannot be tested by the senses: a dwelling in heaven, a future judgment, a gift of the Spirit.

Another set of statements, indeed, make a nonempirically visible "Christ" the one who will judge (5:10), the one whose love constrains (5:14), in whom there is a new creation (5:17), and who reconciles (5:18). God is "in" Christ making reconciliation (5:19). For the sake of Christ, Paul makes appeal (5:20), and "in him" we are made God's righteousness (5:21). Christ is the implied subject of this narrative segment: "and he died in behalf of all, so that those who are living might no longer live for themselves but for the one who died and who was raised for them" (5:15); here, Christ does the dying, and God is the (implied) agent of his being "raised up."

Direct agency is attributed to God (*theos*) in the following statements: the heavenly dwelling is "from God" (5:1); God gave humans the pledge that is the Holy Spirit (5:5); human actions and dispositions are "before God" (5:11, 13); humans can be reconciled to God (5:20) and become God's righteousness (5:21). All things are from God (*ek tou theou*, 5:18); God was in Christ (5:19); God made (Christ) sin (5:21).

In this context perhaps most striking is the presence of a set of statements that are explicitly cognitive in character, with the subject of the statements being Paul and his associates. Thus, while Paul declares that we walk by faith rather than knowledge (5:7), he also claims a certain kind of knowledge shared by himself and his associates: "We know that we have been given a heavenly dwelling" (5:1). We know that when we are clothed with the body, we are away from the Lord (5:6). We know the fear of the Lord (5:11). And we have made the judgment (*krinantas*) that since "one died for all, therefore all have died" (5:14). Most elaborately, "Consequently, from now on we regard [know] no one according to the flesh; even if we once knew Christ according to the flesh, yet we now know him so no longer" (5:16). With such statements, Paul places the intersection of divine and human agency within a distinctive understanding of reality that is shared among those he includes within his "we." By no means does he suggest that such a perception of reality is shared by all: those who see Christ "according to the flesh," for example, will not share the judgment that "he died in behalf of all" and was raised by God (5:15), but would see the death of Jesus as either foolish or scandalous, the death of one "cursed by God" (1 Cor. 1:18–25; 12:3; Gal. 3:13).

Paul's Letters suggest that mythic language is necessary for the faithful to declare even the most basic convictions of faith. Stating that "Christ died for all" and that "God raised him from the dead" belongs not to historical discourse but to mythical discourse. Christians do well to embrace such language enthusiastically, for without it they must remain mute concerning the truths by which they claim to live. But although Paul's language is plainly mythic in the manner I have defined, it is also unlike the sort of mythic narrative that we associate, say, with *Enuma Elish* or Genesis 6:1–4. Paul does not tell stories of figures of the ancient past with heroic dimensions. He speaks of himself and his associates as he addresses a community he founded, and alludes to a narrative concerning a man who died publicly and violently within the lifetime of himself and his readers. Paul employs mythic language in order to express convictions concerning what is happening now in the empirical realm that he shares with his readers.

Can we uncover the logic of such mythic statements about present circumstances and appreciate the way in which they made sense to Paul and his readers? We can approach the question by means of analogy, by examining statements that take the form of an abbreviated narrative and escape any real empirical verification, statements that have some basis in an actual (verifiable) event but transcend what could be demonstrated about that event. Take for example a widow of one of the men who rushed the cockpit of Flight 93 on September 11, 2001, when the airplane had been taken over by terrorists; he was killed together with all aboard that flight when the plane crashed into a Pennsylvania field. Let us imagine that she tells the son who never knew his father, "Your daddy was a great patriot. He died for his country."

71

There is some historical basis for her declaration: her husband actually did die in an effort to save lives: those who rushed the cockpit had learned, we know from their cell-phone communications to loved ones, of the terrorists' mission to use the plane as a weapon of mass destruction. But it is obviously impossible to verify anything about her spouse's motivations or dispositions at the critical moment. Perhaps he lingered reluctantly at the back of the group that rushed the cockpit. Perhaps he vomited in fear at the moment the rush began. His widow's statement to her son does not rely, however, on the determination of such things. It is based instead on her experience and knowledge of her deceased husband, the kind of man she knew him to be. Her judgment is based on something real beyond the brute facts of the historical event. Her statement places his action within the framework of national identity, in which "patriotism" is, from the time of the Roman poet Horace onward, most fully expressed by dying for one's country (*Odes* 3.2.13). Her language elevates the sacrificial act of her husband by placing it within a more public and value-laden symbolic world.

Take another and more ambiguous example: Let us suppose that an Irish-Catholic father reassures his children when his harried wife lashes out irritably while cooking dinner on a hot July day, "Your mother is a saint. You know she would do anything for you children." In this case, the wife's present behavior is negative rather than positive: she manifests anger toward her family. Is the father's interpretation therefore false, a distortive cover-up of bad manners? Not necessarily. First, he invokes a frame of reference both he and the children share: saints are those who show heroic love toward others. Second, in the case of the frazzled mother, the father reminds his children that cooking their supper is one among a multitude of ways that her love is in service to them. Indeed, he suggests, there is no real limit to her love or its practical expression: thus the anger is brought on by fatigue. Third, the experience of her temporary flash of anger is subsumed by an appeal to the mother's overall character, which has been demonstrated by repeated acts of service to the family, acts the children also have come to know. Fourth, the father speaks authoritatively on the basis of his privileged understanding of his wife's character, based on his longer and more intimate experience of her.

72

Such homely examples are only analogies, and weak ones at that. These statements are not "mythic" according to my definition:

they do not assign agency to divine powers. There is a great distance between stating that a father died for his country and stating that Christ died for all humans, so that all have died. There is a similarly great distance between asserting that one's wife is a saint (of sorts) and asserting that God was in Christ reconciling the world. Nevertheless, the examples provide us a sense of how mythic language concerning the present has a definite logic. It is based on a certain kind of personal experience and the subjective knowledge derived from such experience; it involves a judgment concerning the character of the action and its agent; it demands a symbolic framework within which such experience makes sense. In the case of Paul's statement "God was in Christ" (2 Cor. 5:19), we seek an experience commensurate with that claim, a judgment concerning the character of God and Christ, and an understanding of the world within which such predication makes sense.

If we return to our passage in 2 Corinthians 5, we see that the context for Paul's statement "God was in Christ" contains abundant evidence for all three elements. First, the experience: when Paul states in 5:5 that the one who works in him and his associates to prepare them for a heavenly habitation is the God who has given them the pledge that is the Holy Spirit, he echoes a statement he made earlier in the letter: "God is the one who has secured us with you into Christ [*eis Christon*] and has anointed [*chrisas*] us. And he has sealed us and has given us the pledge that is the Holy Spirit in our hearts" (2 Cor. 1:21–22). For Paul, the experience of the presence and power of God ("in our hearts") is in and through Christ, an experience of power that "anoints" Paul and others, giving them a participation (pledge) in Christ's presence. They have a "fellowship in the Holy Spirit" (2 Cor. 13:13), which mediates their "fellowship with Jesus Christ" (1 Cor. 1:9; cf. other statements re the Holy Spirit in 2 Cor. 3:3–18; 4:13; 6:6; 11:4; 12:18).

In turn, this powerful personal experience of God's Holy Spirit through Christ grounds the judgment that Paul shares with his readers concerning Jesus' apparently shameful death by legal execution—a negative historical fact if ever there was one! Paul and his fellows "have reached the judgment" [*krinontas*] concerning Jesus' death (2 Cor. 5:14): it was not a death cursed by God (Deut. 21:23; Gal. 3:13), but a sacrifice undertaken for all, indeed, an expression of love "for us" (2 Cor. 5:14). "He died in behalf of all, so that those who are living might no longer live for themselves but for the sake

73

of the one who died and was raised in their behalf" (5:15). We note that not only Jesus' death but also his resurrection are interpreted as being for the sake of Paul and his readers. Jesus' exaltation to God's right hand, Paul has declared in 1 Corinthians 15:45, made him "life-giving Spirit" (*pneuma zōopoioun*) in such fashion that the existence of Christ and believers are inextricably linked: "We know that the one raising the Lord Jesus will raise us also together with him and place us with you in his presence" (2 Cor. 4:14).

Participation in the Spirit coming from Christ therefore means also human participation in the pattern of his existence, as Paul declares in 2 Corinthians 6:9: "We are as people dying, and behold, we live!" Even when believers receive a sentence of death, they put their trust "in the God who raises the dead" (1:9). If Christ's death on the cross is experienced by others as life, and if his weakness is experienced by others as power, then the presence of the creating God is at work in such a fundamental way that the judgment follows, "If anyone is in Christ, there is a new creation" (5:17), and with it comes a cognitive reevaluation of everything that appears as empirically real: our true home is in heaven, not on earth (5:1–2); when we are in the body, we are far from our home (5:6); when we suffer and groan, it is because we long for heaven (5:2); and when God made Christ to be sin (through a death that Torah declared cursed by God), it was so that we might become "God's righteousness in him" (5:21).

Paul's Letters show how the experience of a resurrection Spirit out of an empirical death demands the use of mythic language, is the only possible means of expressing the truth, impels a reshaping of the symbolic world structuring the reality of his fellow Jews, and demands proclamation to the world of a new paradigm of power-in-weakness that is the sign of God's reconciling presence in creation. The use of such mythic language is no less the necessary means of expressing the experience of God's power and presence in miracles.

Paul also suggests the manner in which mythic language can be tested. Although he claims to have worked the signs of an apostle among his readers, "in signs and wonders and powerful deeds" (2 Cor. 12:12), he insists that it is his character that demonstrates the genuineness of his ministry: his meekness, his lowliness, his weakness, which corresponds to the way in which God has reconciled the world to himself. In contrast, the "superapostles" who

74

so impress the Corinthians are as deceptive as the serpent who deceived Eve; they can be shown to be false by the way in which they peddle a "different Jesus, different good news, different spirit" (11:1–4). Paul's readers, in turn, are tested by the ways in which they are able to distinguish between true and false instantiations of the gospel and then display the character traits that are consistent with the way God has acted in Christ (13:1–10; Stegman 2005). By extension, we can conclude that the only genuine test of mythic language or the genuineness of miracles is the degree to which they correspond to the character of God as revealed in Jesus Christ, and the degree to which they support a life "worthy of God" (1 Thess. 2:12).

In this chapter, I have proposed four elements required to reframe the dominant way of speaking about miracles in a pervasively secularized world: (1) recovering the ability to imagine the world that Scripture imagines, (2) embracing a robust theology of creation, (3) appreciating revelation as a process of human experience and interpretation, and (4) recognizing the distinctive truth-telling capacity of myth. I have also suggested that such reframing requires the most strenuous and consistent efforts of the community of faith to resist double-mindedness and recover the purity of heart that enables it to perceive and celebrate God's powerful presence not only in the words of Scripture from the past but also in the experiences of humans in the present.

PART TWO

God's Presence and Power in the Old Testament

CHAPTER 4

The Mighty Acts of God

Our examination of God's presence and power in creation through miracles now turns explicitly to the texts of Scripture, beginning with the Old Testament. In the stories, songs, and prophecies composed by God's faithful over the long history of Israel, we find not only many accounts of miracles, but above all the shaping of the imaginative world that enables the perception of God as continuously active within his creation. Neither here nor in the following chapters should the reader expect a full analysis—much less an "explanation"—of every individual account. I seek rather to provide a sense of how language about the mighty works of God arises out of real human experience of the world and in turn helps enable such experience within the world.

The convictions for which I argued in part 1 continue here as I turn to an explicit engagement with Scripture. First, the reality of God's miraculous power in the Bible must be considered together with that same power displayed in the contemporary world: if God worked such wonders then, he continues to do so now; conversely, if he does not so work now, neither is it plausible that he did so then. Clearly I hold the first position: the perception of the world as permeable to God's presence and power now both illumines and is illumined by the accounts of God found in Scripture. Second, our engagement with Scripture must take place not at the level of historical verification, even if such were possible, but at the level of imaginative construction. Third, a truly robust appreciation of God's creative activity is the fundamental component of the world thus imagined by Scripture. Fourth, revelation is a process of human interpretation within which the "experience" of God is conditioned by the capacities of those having that experience, not least with respect to the symbols making such experience meaningful. Fifth, mythic language is the necessary vehicle for expressing such human experience of reality, and it needs to be enthusiastically embraced, not only for our view of the Bible but also for our view of the world we experience every day.

The natural and necessary starting point are the songs and stories relating the grand narrative that extends from cosmic and human beginnings, through the call of the patriarchs, the liberation of Israel from Egypt, the giving of torah and the establishment of the cult, to the conquest of the land and the fortunes of the monarchy, the exile, and restoration of the people.

There are some fairly obvious points of similarity between this collection of stories and those gathered into the Greek epic poems the *Iliad* and the *Odyssey*. Just as those epics were ascribed to the single author Homer, even though they represented the activity of countless rhapsodes, so were the stories of the Pentateuch attributed to Moses, even though they arose from diverse oral and written sources. Just as the Greek epics dealt with events of a distant past that had at best a small basis in historical fact, so do the stories of Israel have widely various groundings in verifiable history, ranging from the relatively firm facts concerning the monarchy to the impossible-to-verify accounts of the patriarchs. Just as the Homeric poems provided an etiological basis for Greek values (war, rhetoric, piety, hospitality), so do the stories of Israel's beginnings account for the origins of cities and music and marriage and many nations, as well as the persistent presence of sin, suffering, and violence in families. And just as the Greek epics involve the gods directly and intimately in the lives of their human characters, so that they are properly termed mythological, so the biblical accounts are properly considered mythic in character when God and God's agents are portrayed as acting in the same empirical realm as human characters.